Semen Secrets

Truths and Confessions of a Wife's Journey Through Male Infertility

By: TJ Peyten

Copyright © 2018 GoldenSphinx, LLC

All rights reserved. No part of this book may be reproduced or used in any manner without written permission of the author, except for the use of quotations in a book review.

Printed in the United States of America

Mailing address: PO Box 1592 Norcross GA, 30091

Website: www.semensecrets.com

Cover design ©2018 David Castro
David@davidjcastro.com

Editing by Simone Adams
www.simonewrites.com

ISBN 978-1-7328197-2-6

Disclaimer: This book is the author's personal, non-fictional story. Every account in the book is true, and the events are portrayed to the best of the author's memory. While all the stories in this book are true, names and identifying details were eliminated to protect the privacy of the people involved. This book is not intended to be a substitute for the medical advice of a licensed physician or health professional. The reader should consult with their doctor or other health professional in any matters relating to his/her health. The author does not assume and hereby disclaims any liability to any party for any loss, damage, emotional distress, or disruption as a result of the book content.

BFF Publishing House is a Limited Liability Corporation dedicated wholly to the appreciation and publication of children and adults for the advancement of diversification in literature.

For more information on publishing contact

Antionette Mutcherson at
bff@bffpublishinghouse.com
Website: bffpublishinghouse.com
Published in the United States by
BFF Publishing House
Tallahassee, Florida First Edition, 2018

This book is dedicated to

My husband for allowing me to share this personal story.
It is your patience and kindness that makes this story worth telling.

My children-to-be, TJ and Peyten.
I can't wait for the day I can hold you in my arms.

My family and friends who have supported us along this journey.
We wouldn't have been strong enough to do this alone.

All couples who have experienced infertility and their children-to-be.
You are not alone.

Semen Secrets

Truths and Confessions of a Wife's Journey Through Male Infertility

By: TJ Peyten

Contents

Foreword   10

Introduction   12

Truth 1: The Song Lied   14

Truth 2: Semen Grief is Real   21

Truth 3: Secret Pain Always Tells   29

Truth 4: Unexplainable is Unacceptable   39

Truth 5: Infertile Females are Favorites   47

Truth 6: Modern Medicine Isn't Magic   51

Truth 7: "Just Adopt"	60
Truth 8: Baby Showers Bring Storms	64
Truth 9: Husband Hatred Happens	67
Truth 10: Admit Anger at God	70
Truth 11: Sharing is Caring	78
Truth 12: Grief and Mourning are Different	84
Truth 13: Patience is a Virtue	90
Truth 14: Husband before Children... Always	94
Truth 15: Accept Reality	97

Foreword

It is a common misconception that when a couple gets married, the natural progression is to build a life and start a family. Having a baby is something that is expected of married couples. Yet, there are many couples who have difficulty conceiving a child, and some who, despite all the conventions of modern medicine, are *never* able to conceive or bear a child. This involuntary childlessness is a condition known as **infertility**.

The American Pregnancy Association highlights that approximately 10-15% of couples experience infertility. According to the National Institute of Health, in the U.S., about 9% of men and about 11% of women who are of childbearing age experience infertility. Sadly, while both men *and* women can suffer from infertility, most of the literature, support, and information focuses on female infertility. The subject of infertility is, in itself, a difficult and emotionally challenging subject. But, male infertility is so taboo that many couples dealing with the issue often do so in solitude.

The man is traditionally viewed as a pillar of strength and the head of the household, therefore, his inability to conceive a child can be a crushing reality to endure. For the women supporting these men—typically women who do not have fertility issues themselves—coping with the unfulfilled desire to be a mom while being strong for her broken male partner can often seem unbearable. She must deal with his feelings of inadequacy. She must find ways to help heal his pain. But, most pressing, she must keep his secret.

The woman wants to be there for her husband, to support his needs. She wants to be a woman of faith. She wants her marriage to withstand any challenges. She wants to fix the problem. She wants to fix him. She wants to believe that it does not matter if they never have children because their commitment was not built on that contingency. But, how can she hide her own desire for a child? How long can she continue to suppress the anger, frustration, and disappointment of knowing that her husband is the source of their barrenness, that he is the killer of their dream?

The mystery of infertility can cause the wife to question her faith and all that she believes. Her strength and her faith begin to falter. Her hope and optimism begin to fade. What did they do wrong as a couple? Is this some type of punishment? What's the point of being married if she cannot have a baby? Why didn't she know this *before* she said, "I do?"

As the weeks, months, and even years pass without a child, the wife may begin to give up on her dreams. It can take her down the road of depression. Although she'll never admit it, it can make her bitter and jealous of friends who seem to conceive so easily. Worse, it can make her hate the one she vowed to love in sickness and in health.

This book explores male infertility through the eyes of the wife, *me*. This is my experience as a young, loving wife and the agony of not being able to have children while trying to understand how to temper those feelings and support my husband, who was unable to give me the children we wanted. My story details how semen can keep a secret that, once told, leads to a series of tumultuous events and emotions, turning friends into enemies, lovers into fighters, and hopes into dashed dreams. This is the story of me and my husband, our journey through infertility to a place of self-discovery, revealing the weaknesses and the true strength of our relationship, the conviction of our faith, our unconditional love, and our ability to persevere through adversity.

Introduction

Now, of course, semen can't talk, but what if I told you my husband's semen had a secret—information it had been hiding for decades. Unlike the semen of other men, my husband's semen did not contain any sperm. Zero. Nada. Nothing.

As defined by Merriam-Webster

Semen /ˈsēmən/ (noun) A viscid whitish fluid of the male reproductive tract consisting of spermatozoa (sperm) suspended in secretions of accessory glands

Secret /ˈsē-krət/ (noun) Something kept hidden or unexplained: a mystery

Truth /ˈtrüth/ (noun) The body of real things, events, and facts: Actuality; the state of being the case: Fact

Confession /kən-ˈfe-shən/ (noun) A written or oral acknowledgment of guilt by a party accused of an offense

I define these four words as they outline the events of our infertility journey. The Semen—that was the catalyst that started it all. The Secrets of the semen turned out to be lies we told ourselves about how this whole idea of conception and becoming parents were supposed to work. The Truths are what I learned once I discovered the lies, and the Confessions are my reflections of the journey where I had to own my truth. I found that the Semen Secrets forced me to deal with more than just infertility—they forced me to deal with me.

Like most secrets, once told this secret changed the course of my life. Most of the time, I dealt with the secrets in silence. But in the following pages, I will finally share the emotions that I've been dealing with alone.

My hope is that the secrets and truths and confessions you'll find in this book will help you to understand that male infertility isn't just a clinical diagnosis, nor is it a condemnation sentence, it's merely an obstacle that a husband and wife must face—together.

Truth 1: The Song Lied

Semen Secret: The formula is simple: fall in love and find a husband so you can have a house, a car, a job, a dog, and a baby.

First comes love, then comes marriage, then comes the baby in the baby carriage... It was a simple nursery rhyme I sang as a child, but I was conditioned to believe those lines were a formula for life.

My husband and I grew up in church together, but if you would have told me he was going to be my husband, my response would have been, "who is he again?" Fast forward to my junior year in high school, when he just happened to need a date for his prom and I just happened to have a friend who went to his school and didn't want to go to prom with her date alone. Long story short and sweet, we both agreed to be each other's date to prom, albeit reluctantly. Ironically, or perhaps, divinely, what began as a mercy date turned into a great night. He was a sweet guy who I'd known since I was six, but that night got a chance to meet the young man he had become, and I liked what I saw. I later learned that after our date I stayed on his mind. He asked my friend to ask me if he could give me a call, "you know, to talk… I just got her number for prom… not to call her on the regular." It was a weird request (he could have just called me), but I respected his old-fashioned romanticism.

We quickly became high school sweethearts. He was the picture of chivalry—asking my parent's permission before asking me on dates, bringing flowers, opening doors. He reminded me of my dad, gentle and compassionate. Not to mention, he was handsome, well-spoken, and voted best-dressed his senior year in high school. He always made me feel that I was special, like I was the only girl in the world. I didn't know what love was at the time, but I knew, even at 17 years old, that I felt a spark for him that I didn't feel with anyone else.

In our senior year, he said, quite matter-of-factly, "God said you are going to be my wife." Of course, there was a pause and that stare you give when someone has just spoken foolishness to you. I loved him, but marriage? I hadn't even decided what I wanted to be in life. I sarcastically replied, "Well, he hasn't told me that, and we talk every day." I laughed it off, but he was serious. From that day on, he took every chance he could to let me know that what he and God had talked about was supposed to be true.

Despite his affirmation from God, it took six years of dating (yes six!) before he got down on one knee to ask me to be his wife. And I didn't hesitate to say yes. I couldn't have written a better story if I tried.

We were in our early twenties—the first in our group of friends to tie the knot. Being a young married couple with our whole future ahead of us, we made the decision to wait to have children. We had time. We were the best of friends, but we still wanted to get to know each other, travel, build our careers, and simply get adjusted to being husband and wife.

After four years of marriage, we eventually decided that we would start trying to have a baby. The following year would mark our five-year anniversary and most of the people we knew were now getting married and having kids. Not to mention, friends and family had started asking the inevitable question... *When are y'all going to have a baby?*

In my mind, I would have my first baby just before I turned 30 and my last baby by the age of 33. We would still be young enough to run behind our kids, and so would our parents. For me, that was very important. My husband had one grandmother still living, our other grandparents died, either before we got to know them or just as we were getting old enough to understand the blessing of having a grandparent. For our kids to have both sets of grandparents alive would be a blessing for everyone.

I had been on birth control for a considerable amount of time because I had issues with ovarian cysts and fibroids since my teen years, which the pills helped suppress. My doctor felt it was important that I give my body time to adjust to not being on birth control so we could start a family. He suggested it might take six months to a year after stopping birth control before I could conceive.

So, February of the year before our fifth anniversary, I swallowed my last birth control pill.

We had heard stories about people immediately getting pregnant after they stopped taking the pill. I had a few false promises of pregnancy because in the beginning, my cycle was unpredictable. It took about three months for my body to re-regulate itself and for my period to become consistent. Because I had used the birth control to help suppress my fibroids and cysts, in July I went back to my doctor to make sure I wasn't having any issues. I knew that fibroids and cysts in my uterus could impede my ability to have a child. However, the doctor assured me that I was healthy and that we should have no problem conceiving our little bundle of joy in the coming year.

We wanted twins, who we had already named TJ and Peyten. Twins ran on both sides of our family and we wanted a boy and a girl to bring into the family.

I turned 29 in March of the next year. It was the year I had termed my "conception" year. I had one year left before I turned 30, one year left before I had to meet my deadline of having my first kid. I counted backwards nine months from my 30th birthday and realized that I was already running out of time. Every time my period came it served as a reminder that my deadline was arbitrary. I bought pregnancy tests and used ovulation calculators as if they would help the process along. Nothing helped. By the summer of my conception year, I was annoyed and a little concerned that we hadn't yet conceived. I was taking pregnancy tests even before my period was late, hoping for a positive.

I feared my cysts and fibroids were preventing me from conceiving. We visited my doctor again and as he started asking questions about our ability to have a baby I started to panic. It had always been in the back of my mind that cysts and fibroids could change the shape of my uterus, causing miscarriages, or making it difficult to carry a child. I had never shared this fear with my husband, but it had always been there and now he would find out that I was preventing us from having our baby.

"Oh, you're fine," my doctor assured me, and my panic faded. "Remember, it takes a year for most couples to get pregnant."

"Wait? A year? You told me it took a year last year. You meant I need a year to be off birth control and then another whole year to try and have a baby?"

What about my plan, my timeline? I assumed we were supposed to have wild sex one minute and the next month I would take a pee test, get the plus sign, and we would be decorating TJ and Peyten's nursery... right?

My doctor saw my anguish and patted my shoulder, "Yes, a year or more. But, if you just want to make sure that there is nothing going on, your husband can go get checked out."

My husband shot the doctor the look like, *What the hell could be wrong with me*? For men, especially black men, the idea of something not performing up to par in the male reproductive area was taboo.

"I don't wanna waste the money for me to get checked, but okay, if it will get you to leave me alone," my husband answered in a cocky, nonchalant manner.

It was settled. The doctor would check his semen, he would be fine, and we would soon meet our little replicas.

More than a year and a half after I took my last birth control pill, almost six months after our doctor assured me my reproductive system was fine, and only two weeks after the semen analysis, I got a call from the lab. I was working from home and answered the phone, expecting good news.

Nurse: Hello, how are you?

Me: I'm great.

Nurse: Well, I was calling to give you the results of your husband's test.

Me: Yes. What did you find?

Nurse: Well… we didn't find anything.

Me: See, I knew there was nothing to worry about. My doctor had us all worried.

Nurse: Well, uh, no, you see, we didn't find anything. We didn't find any sperm.

Me: What? What do you mean no sperm? Like what, you mean you lost it?

Nurse: No, we spun it down several times and there was no sperm in the ejaculate. I'm very sorry. We'll send the results back to your doctor. Your husband should do a follow-up exam to determine the cause.

Me: But wait, wait, what does this mean? I don't understand. All men have sperm.

Nurse: I'm sorry. You'll have to talk with your doctor. I only have the lab results.

I stared at the phone. I felt like I had been punched in the chest, like the wind had been knocked out of me. I felt tears welling up and a knot in my throat that made it difficult to talk.

Nurse: Are you there? Are you okay?

Me: I… I don't know. I… I… thank you. I'll follow-up with the doctor.

I hung up the phone. My head felt so heavy that I couldn't see straight. *No sperm? How could that be? And what did it mean for the plan?*

All I could think about was the plan, my precious plan. *I am supposed to have children. By 30! We are supposed to have children. We followed the formula—we dated first, then we got married, and now we're supposed to have a baby. How can my husband not have any sperm?*

I was screaming at the walls with tears streaming down my face. My head was throbbing. I couldn't catch my breath. My world, my perfect world, was crumbling. I was so confused that I hadn't yet registered the pain—only the disappointment. No baby? That meant failure, and I didn't know what failure looked like. People looked at us as the ideal couple. Our parents were counting on us to give them grandchildren. Questions swirled in my head and I couldn't keep up with my own thoughts. *What will people think? What will people say? Will I ever be a mommy?* Imperfection was foreign to me and, in my mind, my husband and I were perfect.

I thought back to all the movies from fifth-grade sex ed about puberty and what happens when you have sex. I felt like everything I had ever known to be true was a lie. The damn semen lied to me.

I guess it didn't lie… it just held secrets. Secrets that would forever change my life, his life, our lives.

CONFESSION: Love + Marriage ≠ Baby. The reality was slowly settling in that my "baby in the baby carriage" was only the lyric to a children's song. My husband and I followed what we thought was the formula: we dated, got married, and *then* decided to start our family. But none of that mattered. All my life I had believed that men make sperm and women make eggs. The sperm swims to the egg and presto! We have babies. I wasn't prepared for the unthinkable, for the idea that I may never be able to recreate myself, never carry out my family lineage, never procreate with the man I love.

I agonized over the pain of unmet expectations. The sad truth is that I was never promised any of those expectations.

Truth 2: It Felt Like Death

Semen Secret: You can only grieve over the death of a person, or maybe even a pet.

When people die, their loved ones grieve. But, in my case, no one died.

A few hours after I hung up with the nurse at the lab, the phone rang again. It was my husband. I had been screaming and crying so much that there was no disguising the anguish in my voice.

"What's wrong? Did the doctor say something bad?"

I hesitated, "Well, I think we should wait until you get home to talk about this."

"What do you mean?" I could hear the panic in his voice, "Just tell me now. It can't be that bad. What is it? I only have a few thousand sperm instead of a million?"

"I just think we should talk about this at home."

"I got to get back to work. Just tell me!" He was trying not to raise his voice, but his frustration was apparent.

I tried to fight back the tears, but they streamed down my face. Choking, I said, "You don't … you don't have any have sperm."

"Huh?"

I cleared my throat, "I said they didn't find any sperm, not one. Your semen didn't have any."

There was a long pause, as if time stood still.

"Are you going to be okay?" I asked, "I'm so sorry. We can just pray and—"

"Please," he interrupted. "It's okay. I'm good. I'll see you when I get home."

For the next several hours I sat alone in silence. My mom called to chat. It was our usual routine, only this time while I was talking, I was still shrouded in silence because I couldn't hear the words I was speaking. She said I sounded strange. I told her I had a lot going on with work. I didn't know how to tell my mom that she may not have grandchildren from her only daughter.

I waited for the nurse to call me back to tell me it was a mistake. She never did. I went over her words again and again. *No sperm*. Each time it made tears swell, and I felt a terrible loss of the visions and dreams I had for my family, the plan, our baby. I tried to imagine what I would say to my husband when he got home. Would I grab him and tell him I love him and I'm sorry? Would we cry together? Would I accuse him of ruining our perfect lives? Would I say nothing at all? I wasn't sure what he would need from me, but in all honesty, I had nothing to give.

When my husband came home that evening, he walked in the door like our world was still right-side-up. He put down his bag, looked at the mail, used the bathroom, washed his hands, and went in the fridge to get a snack. I was confused and angry. Here I was agonizing about how I was going to comfort him. We were just told we would never be able to have a child of our own and he felt... *nothing*? I realized that while I was trying to figure out how to comfort him, I needed him to comfort me. I wanted him to run in and take me in his arms and cry with me until we were spent and exhausted. I would have accepted him yelling in a furious rage, ranting about the unfairness of the situation. But I couldn't understand him not having a reaction.

Finally, we sat down at the kitchen table to talk through the unspeakable. I had to repeat it more than once in my mind before the words would come out of my mouth: "She said they didn't find any sperm. The doctor wants to set up an appointment with you to go over everything."

His response was immediate, "Well, I don't want to go. I don't want to. I don't have any sperm. That's it. You want a baby. I can't do that, so that's it."

That's it? That's it? What do you mean? I began to rock back and forth, shaking my head in disbelief. I looked away trying to hide my hurt and anger as tears began to swell in the corner of my eyes. I wanted to grab him and tell him that I wasn't going to give up so easily. I wanted to bang on the table, stand up in the chair, and scream until my throat burned. *We don't quit! That's not it for me! That's not it for us. Damn it, you gotta have something in there. I just won't believe it.*

Instead, I said, "But I didn't marry you just for a baby." Although I did expect that was part of the package, "I married you because I love you. You're my best friend, not just my husband. So, don't say that."

Before I could finish, the tears that had been building since he walked through the door were flowing down my cheeks. If he wasn't going to cry, I was. They were not silent, sad tears. These tears were heavy with loss and confusion and regret and anger and hurt and a myriad of other feelings I hadn't yet identified. My chest heaved, and my head ached. My shoulders shook with the sobs and my face was distorted with all the emotion I couldn't voice.

My husband's face softened, he reached his hand across the table to comfort me. "Okay," he said in a whisper. "I'll go to the follow-up appointment with the doctor," and then he added, more firmly, "but then we are done with it."

For the remainder of the night, we moved in an awkward silence that was so loud I couldn't stand it. I drew myself a warm bath and played soft music hoping to reason my way out of this situation, or at least find solace. I stayed in the water until my skin was milky and shriveled, still I had no answers. I wanted to talk to someone who could help me make sense of this or at least offer me the sympathy my husband couldn't. But also, I couldn't imagine telling anyone. It felt so shameful. *We are supposed to have children. Why us? Why him? Why me?*

The next morning came and I wasn't ready to face the day, let alone work. I was worlds away. I kept replaying the phone call in my head. *No sperm.* That night my husband and I moved in silence again. We avoided each other. When he came to the kitchen, I went to the couch. Instead of watching our favorite shows together, we watched them in separate rooms. When it was time for dinner we tried to make small talk.

"How was work today?"

"Did you get a chance to go to the store this afternoon?"

Eventually, the conversation felt so forced that we stared at our plates and stuffed our faces so could get up from the table and resume ignoring each other.

All I could envision was the way we use to laugh and cuddle with one another, follow each other from room to room so we could talk about the day—that was just two days ago. I knew love didn't fade away that fast, but at that moment my husband felt like a stranger.

After dinner, I went outside and cried. It was a cool night and I sat alone under the stars with a glass of wine and some music to keep me company. The salt of the tears mixed with my wine. I kept imaging the life I wanted: us going to the ultrasound, him feeling the baby kick in my stomach, how our parents would react when we told them we were having a baby. I pictured the hospital room—him holding my hand telling me to push. I looked in the backyard and could see the swing set and us running around the yard playing with our child.

I tried to convince myself that I was being silly crying over semen, over sperm, or the lack thereof. Those little things that were to carry our DNA did not exist for us. Our children did not exist. I grieved over his semen, my empty womb, our marriage, and our non-existent children, but also the death of my husband's bright spirit. The light in his eyes grew dim. He became a stranger to himself, to me. I knew he struggled with his thoughts of manhood, but he refused to speak about it. I wanted to help him, to fix it, to fix us. I watched his spirit slip away without understanding how to help him. I wanted to talk about it (as most women do), but he dismissed me every time. And as helpless as I felt, I was also angry that he didn't try to fix me. I needed him to help me understand all of this. He always helped me figure out what was next. Where was *that* guy when I needed him?

The third night after the call, my husband rolled over in the bed and tapped me gently on my shoulder. I turned towards him, relieved that he was ready to talk. I had longed for his touch and I was eager to embrace him, for us to comfort each other and cry in each other's arms.

"I don't think I want to have sex anymore with you. I want a divorce," He said flatly.

I sprang up in the bed, "What? Why?"

Propping up on his pillow, he took a deep breath and explained, "I know you want kids. I can't give that to you, and I love you enough to let you go find someone who can do that for you. I'll be fine."

"But, I've told you, I didn't marry you for your sperm. I married you for you. Do I want children? Absolutely. But I want our children, not someone else's. I want to know what we look like. Me and you." There was an urgency in my voice that caused me to tremble.

A knot formed in my throat. I understood he was only trying to protect me, but he was breaking my heart at the same time. Instead, he turned his back to me and looked at the wall "No. I'm straight. I can't live knowing I can't give you what you want."

"You're just angry," I reasoned. "Maybe we should talk to someone, tell our parents."

"No!" He shouted, turning back to face me so I understood how serious he was, "I'm not telling anybody my dick don't work! And, you can't tell anyone either. It's my issue, not yours."

"Well, I'm not going to leave you, especially not when you need me."

"Like I said," he turned his back again, "this is my issue. You can have a baby with someone else. I can't."

My tears came quickly. The knot moved from my throat to my chest, making it difficult for me to say anything in response. When I found my voice, I told him repeatedly that I loved him and that I wouldn't leave. My pleas fell on deaf ears and he finally rolled over, pulled up the covers, and turned out the light. I sat in that dark room sobbing. I knew he didn't mean what he was saying. I knew he was hurt, but so was I. I wanted to be a mom but that was taken away from me, and there was nothing I could do about it. I wiped my nose with my pajama shirt sleeve and looked up at the fan, focusing on the hum of the blades. It calmed me, and the coolness dried some of my tears.

Without warning, I had gone from being a wife and a hopeful mom to a childless divorcee. I didn't know if my husband and I were actually growing apart or if we just didn't know how to handle this situation. I listened to my husband's rhythmic breathing and wondered if he was asleep or lying awake like I was. I couldn't imagine a life without him. The more I considered his threat to divorce me, the more panicked I became until I couldn't lie in the bed anymore. I got up and ran to the basement where I could cry without him hearing me.

For the next few weeks, we barely spoke to each other. He didn't bring up the divorce and neither did I, but I walked on eggshells for fear that if I asked him to talk to me he would act on his words. I desperately wanted to know what he was thinking. He was my buddy, and I was his. We needed each other, even if the tension made us feel as if we didn't.

I was furious with him, but then I also felt a tenderness towards him. Even though he wouldn't admit it, I knew he was as hurt and scared as I was. But my understanding his feelings didn't mean that I was ready to forgive his words. I was already mourning the idea of not having a child, now I also feared losing my husband. I couldn't wrap my thoughts around why, of all people, this was happening to us. I hadn't understood how devoted I was to the idea of having children and raising a family, until the option was taken away. I hadn't even fully comprehended that the option wasn't a possibility before I was in jeopardy of losing my marriage too. Losing the children I had only dreamed of was terrible, but losing my husband was unthinkable. In a few days, I had gone from a happily married woman to a madwoman grieving children who hadn't yet been conceived and my once enviable marriage was on the verge of ruin.

I was alone. I wanted someone to blame, someone to be angry at, someone to cry with, someone to make it all go away. But each day, the reality of the issue caused a roller coaster of shoulda-woulda-couldas, why me, why him, why us, why not, I will be fine, we will be okay, this is only temporary, maybe it's not in the plan, and to hell with all the people walking around with babies who were unfit to be parents. I deserved a baby, we deserved a baby. And yet, we couldn't conceive a baby.

CONFESSION: I had only associated grief with the loss of the living, but what I was feeling felt like a death. I grieved over an idea—the idea that we would be parents, that I would be a mother and he would be a father. After one semen analysis, that idea died. However, there was no funeral, no memorial, no tombstone, no place we could visit, and no one to share our loss. Our grief was private. We grieved our ability to conceive our own children, and the feeling was suffocating. We were both losing our light, dying on the inside, but we had to be alive and well for the world on the outside. Living a lie of happiness was a death unto itself.

I came to realize that what I was grieving over was not the semen itself, but my unmet expectations. I suffered the embarrassment of not being able to have a child naturally. I feared facing a world that looked to my husband and I as a couple who had it all together and having to admit that we didn't have it all. I was afraid of what people would say, what people would think. My ego took a huge blow, my pride was crushed. My grief had nothing to do with my child or my husband. My grief was that my perfect world was imperfect, and I was not equipped to deal with imperfection.

Truth 3: Secret Pain is Never Kept

Semen Secret: Keep your problems to yourself. You're too embarrassed to tell anyone your shortcomings, and your husband is too fragile for you to expose his lack of what he refers to as "manhood."

I felt alone, but I hadn't dared to reach out to anyone to comfort me. I stayed isolated. I kept my husband's secret while I mourned our marriage and our happiness. My loneliness and grief were compounded by my husband's stubbornness and unwillingness to talk. He expected that my grief should mirror his own but the silence, the inability to purge or process my thoughts, was compounding my grief. I had to tell someone. It was too much to carry on my own. I was willing to betray my husband's confidentiality to calm my suffering.

I confided in my sister-in-law first. Though she and my brother were no longer together, she had always been a reliable confidant, letting me cry about silly things or vent about critical issues. I needed her calm demeanor and level head to help me through this thing I couldn't understand.

"Hello," My voice cracked.

"What's wrong? You sound upset."

I didn't even try to hold back, I let go of everything that I had been holding inside.

"I can't… I can't have a baby," I shouted into the phone. "He doesn't have any sperm. It's so unfair. I won't be a mom. I'll never know what it's like. I just don't know why God would do this to me. Me? Why? Why would He do this to me?"

I continued shouting and pounded my fingers to my chest, accepting the personal defeat until finally, the levy broke inside my soul. I allowed myself to feel all of the pain and loss.

What I appreciate most is that my sister-in-law, who was usually a woman of many words, didn't say a thing. For 45 minutes she stayed on the phone with me and let me cry until I ran out of tears. All she said was, "just get it out and we'll talk about it when you do." Get it out. That's what I needed.

I knew that my husband didn't want me to tell his secret, but I didn't care, at least not at the time the words were coming out of my mouth. However, if he knew I told someone he would feel I had violated his trust, and what I didn't need was another argument on top of everything else we were dealing with. Still, I didn't want to walk around giving him a false sense of security and protection about his condition. At the same time, I was the worst at keeping things from him. He was my husband and my friend. I was torn.

Meanwhile, my husband's anger and depressed state became worse. His communication was short and sarcastic. We argued about everything. Everything we did to or for one another got on the other's nerves.

I was a wreck, but I tried to keep my sanity. My husband, however, let his whole self-image go. The exercising stopped, and he was not social. He would say he was a freak, that something was wrong with him, that he wasn't normal. Then, he would accuse me of being the one who thought those things about him.

"You know you don't want a man who can't have kids," he'd whine.

And I would shout back, "I didn't say shit to you!"

We had always had a loving respect for each other, but we began to hurl curse words at each other as easily as we said good morning. I knew we were both hurting and, as they say, hurt people hurt people. I admit, there were times that I did want to throw it in his face. I thought, *how did you not know you didn't have sperm*? Then again, how would he know if he never tried to have a baby before?

We hadn't had sex since we found out. Neither of us felt like being intimate and I'm sure it would have been impossible not to think about the problem while we were supposed to be focused on pleasing each other. I began to worry that we would never be able to function again as a normal couple.

We were only one month into a treacherous journey, but it already felt like a lifetime. Every day was a new test—the ebb and flow of the stages of grief. We went from denial to anger to depression to bargaining and back to denial again. Somedays I cried, some days I convinced myself it was going to be okay, and other days, like the moment I got another baby shower invitation in the mail, my grief would feel as fresh as it had the first day.

One day my husband came home and I could tell he had been crying.

"I told my parents I couldn't have kids," he started, "They both started crying. My mom asked all these questions. Said it was her fault. She felt like, as a nurse, she should have known. She said I had mumps as a kid, but she took me to the doctor early enough. Said the doctor said he noticed something in my blood work before I went to college, but she never took me back to have it checked. My dad didn't even know what to say. All he could get out was, 'I'm sorry son.' He just couldn't understand. You happy now?" He choked, "I told someone and look what it did to them! I told you I didn't want to tell."

I sat in silence and let him talk because I knew he needed to vent as much as I had when I called my sister-in-law. Plus, it was the most he had shared with me since he told me he wanted a divorce. Him telling his parents solidified for me that he was using divorce as a defense mechanism, an easy way out so he could deal with this on his own and give me a chance at motherhood. But, I wanted motherhood with him and no one else. He went against his own vow not to tell because he felt guilty that he couldn't give me what I wanted and couldn't even tell me why. He was always that way. Trying to give me the world if he could. He had called his parents to try to get answers that they just didn't have.

I wanted to ask dozens of questions, but I knew questions would cause him to shut down. So, I listened. It was okay for him to be upset. I understood that I could not identify with his pain.

Shortly thereafter, I received two separate calls from my husband's parents, both apologizing and wanting to pray with me. Both going through the *what if this* and *what if that* and *if only I had done this* or *that, he would be fine.* They were going to talk to doctors, look at old medical records. But understanding why it happened was water under the bridge at this point. We couldn't go back in time. I knew they meant well but I didn't want to hear what they had to say. In that moment, their "sorry" couldn't erase my sorrow. It made me sadder and my husband even more angry, sad, and frustrated. In retrospect, I didn't even consider that they too were in pain.

The next few days I contemplated if I should tell my parents now that my husband's parents knew. I called my sister-in-law because she was still the only one I could talk to who knew my situation. Once I told her about the weight on my shoulders, she said, "You need to tell your parents. You don't want them to find out from his parents, and you know they talk."

I knew it went against what my husband wanted, but I needed to let my parents know. If they found out from my husband's parents before I told them, they would be heartbroken and feel betrayed. Plus, I needed my parents' support. I wanted some answers and parents were supposed to know everything.

I called my mom and broke the news. I did not cry at first because I knew she would be worried. But as I shared my story, the tears began to pour. Before I knew it, my tears turned in to a complete breakdown.

"You are just going to have to pray," she said. "God knows what's best. You must believe that He will give you the desires of your heart. You know the scripture, 'Write the vision and make it plain.' Remember, I had your name before I ever met your dad and I told people I was going to have a little girl. It wasn't until seven years later that you came into the world, but for seven years I thanked God every day for my daughter. I even brought clothes and shoes for you. People thought I was crazy, but here you are.

So, write it down and don't wavier in your faith."

God? Prayer? Faith? Writing? I had done all that and still nothing changed. *Seven years?* Patience had never been my forte. I wanted to have kids before I was 33—I didn't have that much time. Deep down, her comment made me angry. My mom was supposed to fix it. I simply wanted her to tell me that this would be better tomorrow.

My dad called the next day and repeated the same sentiment, "It will be fine, just pray. Whatever you need, you know we will give it to you to make this happen."

What I needed was my husband to produce sperm. It was clear God wasn't interested in my issue or I wouldn't be having this conversation.

Ultimately, my parents didn't tell me what I wanted to hear.

And I didn't want to hear what my husband would say once I revealed that I had shared his secret. But now that my parents knew and could possibly talk with his parents about it, the time had come for me to spill my own secret.

I picked a time when it was quiet. We were watching TV together. We were on separate couches, but at least we were in the same room.

"Um, so, I told my parents and my sister-in-law about out issues."

He dropped the remote and turned his face toward the wall. He shook his head slowly. I braced myself for the eruption.

"Why did you do that? I don't want pity from your parents. Do you know how it feels to feel like you are the one keeping them from their grandchild? This is my issue. It is my story to tell. You had me tell my parents and that shit was embarrassing. But now this? Who else you wanna tell?"

I tried to reason with him, to see the logic that they would find out from his parents. I tried to get his sympathy, that I needed someone to talk to and it was unfair for me not to be able to tell my parents.

"You're saying it's unfair for me to tell my parents and not tell yours, but it's unfair that this is even an issue."

It was unfair, but I kept asserting that I needed to tell my parents to get my support system. Honestly, I didn't give a damn if he felt some type of way about it. I was already alone in the marriage because he wouldn't talk to me, so I was gonna tell those people who I knew could help me make sure I didn't go off the deep end.

It's hard for a wife to carry the pain of her husband, her own pain, and hold the home up spiritually. It was too much, but life didn't stop to let me grieve this death of a dream. I still had to wake up every morning, go to work every day, smile and chat with friends, and take care of our home.

After I told my parents, my husband wouldn't open up to me again. To him, the issue was a point of embarrassment. I believed that sharing his pain would help him relieve the stress, give him someone to help him work through his issues. But, I was wrong. It made him more reclusive.

The silence was so agonizing, I couldn't bear it. Though I told my mom and my sister-in-law. I needed another outlet. I knew it would again violate my husband's wishes, but my family was too close to me to be objective. I needed another perspective. I decided to pray. *Show me who else I can tell.* I can't say it was in prayer that I got the name or if it was just a decoy to justify my selfish spirit needing to find some way to validate what I was getting ready to do. I needed to share with a friend who would keep my confidence, not place judgement, not pity me or let me wallow in my pain. Mostly, I wanted someone to tell me it was going to be okay. Days passed by and still no answer. Then my best friend from high school called to check on me.

"Hey, girl. You've been on my mind," She began. "Is everything okay?"

I rolled my eyes at the phone. *Is everything okay? Who could be okay?* But, I replied, "Chile yeah, we all good over here."

"Nope, I don't believe you," she stated.

I was her daughter's godmother and I was at her first birthday party about a week ago. Had I been acting strange?

I laughed her statement off, hoping that the questioning would end, but she just kept probing. Finally, I relented and shared my painful story of dreams lost. As I recounted the hurt, the tears came again. She let me cry, then she gave me the same message my parents had offered: pray.

Wiping away my tears and my runny nose, I choked out the word, "Don't you think I'm doing that? I'm never going to be a mom!"

"Every day, there are people who birth babies, but they aren't 'moms'. Being a mother is not contingent on the DNA of you or your husband. There are plenty of adopted kids, sperm donor kids, and even kids in your family who can look to you as a mom. Look how much you love on my baby. You're her godmother and I don't take that lightly. So, do you wanna be a "mom" or do you just want to be pregnant to have that experience? Those are two different things."

I never thought about it like that.

I was sure that if I ever mentioned adoption, my husband's response would be, "I don't wanna raise no one else's child." And, if I was honest with myself, I didn't want to either. For me, sperm donation was out of the question. I think it came from watching too much TV. I imagined getting the sperm of some crazy person and that crazy DNA passing down to my child. The next thing you know I've raised a serial killer. See, too much TV.

What did I really want? What did my husband and I really want?

"Well, no offense," I said, "but you have had a baby. You don't know what it feels like to not be able to have one. You know what you and your husband look like. I want to know that. It's just hard. I don't think anyone understands."

"I can't say I know how you feel. But, I can say that being a mom is so much more than giving birth to a baby. That I do know."

The rational part of me knew she was right, but at the time, I was unwilling to let go of the hurt. It seemed so unfair that everyone around me was having a baby while I was wondering if I would ever experience that joy.

The next week, I felt led to tell my coworker. We were sisters in faith and keepers of each other's sanity at work. I found myself in her office on a day when I was feeling low. It didn't take long for her to ask me what was wrong, and this time I didn't hesitate to share my story.

She interrupted my tears to say, "Are you going to vent and cry or do you want to listen? If you're not ready to hear what I have to say, then I'll shut up and let you finish getting it out of your system."

I hoped she would tell me something different, something no one else had said. "Okay, Okay," I gave in. "Give me some tissue."

She leaned over the desk and spoke in an even tone: "Speak the Word over your life; declaring what God said he would do. My pastor talks about finding people in the Bible like your own story. I am going to have in faith with you. I don't know how you feel because I am a mom but look around you. You still have so much to give, and there is nothing keeping you from having kids. You just want to have kids the way you want to and that might not be what God wants."

This same message again? I sighed.

I relented, "Okay, I'll look in the Bible."

I spent the evening flipping through chapter after chapter. Though I couldn't find anywhere where infertility was the issue for the man. I did find Abraham and Sarah, the great Shunammite woman, and Elisabeth and Zachariah who all faced issues with fertility. Then, I started looking at scripture. Psalms 84:11 and God will not withhold any good thing. Deuteronomy 7:14 and no one being barren. I wrote scriptures about healing and about children being a gift from God. My spirit was lifted.

But my lifted moment was short-lived. By the next week, the anger and grief returned. My husband still wouldn't touch me, and I still didn't want to look at him. I cried every night before going to bed. I woke up angry every morning. I didn't understand why we were plagued with this situation. I wanted someone to blame. God? Did my husband do something and this was punishment? If this did happen in his childhood, why didn't his doctors know?

Thanksgiving arrived and we visited with our parents and extended family, but we weren't ready for the questions. We discovered that to smile through pain is like an out of body experience. Everyone seemed to ask the same question, "When are y'all going to have a baby?" I wanted to shout back, *when you have it for me* or *stay out of my vagina and I'll stay out of yours*. Instead, I replied, "We're not in a rush," or "Whenever God sees fit to bless us."

Our parents looked like they wanted to run over and hug us, but they held our secret. I couldn't fault the people asking the questions. They didn't know better. In another situation, the questions would have been harmless—but on this day, they caused unbearable pain and still, I had to bear it and with a smile on my face. I couldn't wait until we got back home so I could curl up in my own bed and snuggle with my sorrows.

Over the next two weeks, two more people came into my path who I felt like it was okay for me to tell: one of my friends from grad school and a friend of a friend. They were both moms, but I thought they could still be encouraging. Each had the same message. It seemed as if everyone had read the same sermon: pray, have faith, and it will happen. But, my faith continued to falter. Where was my burning bush? Where was the one touch that could heal my husband? All the words started to sound the same, and my situation also remained the same.

The more people I told the secret, the more people who told me lies. I was not having a baby. We were not having a baby. Just like my husband's semen, the words were empty and blank. They did nothing to fill the void in my heart and heal my broken marriage or spirit. Male infertility was new to me. It was my scarlet letter written on my chest and his penis.

CONFESSION: I told the world because I wanted someone to tell me that it was going to be okay. I wanted someone to peek into my heart and put it back in a place where it could beat again. However, the more people who told me it was going to be okay, the more I began to doubt. Everyone I talked to had what I wanted: a baby. No one understood my pain. I was searching in them for something that they were not equipped to give me: peace of mind and a reason why this was happening to him, to me, to us.

Semen Secrets

Truth 4: Unexplainable is Unacceptable

Semen Secret: There are answers for everything. That is why we have doctors, Google, Wikipedia, and God. Out of the four, something or someone is going to be able to explain what is causing your tragedy.

As the reality of our situation settled in, the need to find out what was wrong with my husband became apparent. Everyone in his family seemed to be fertile and, according to his parents, there was no medical issue that they knew of that could cause him to be sperm-less.

I reached out to my primary care doctor who referred us to a urologist. The first appointment was awkward, watching the doctor poke my husband's testicles and exam his penis. I could tell my husband felt uncomfortable. The urologist took some initial notes and ordered a series of blood tests. He told us to come back in a week for a follow-up. *That's it?!* We left disappointed. We expected more. We wanted immediate answers, something to acknowledge the death of our dreams.

The week seemed to last forever, and the follow-up appointment felt like it was a lifetime away. I checked my phone every day hoping the doctor would call and tell us how this secret got started. I needed someone to explain how no one in the whole entire medical stratosphere had ever told my husband that he would never be able to have children. You would think someone would be able to pause and read into the one thing that was off with my husband. Then again, I guess a sperm check wasn't a requirement until your wife wanted to have a baby.

Finally, it was the day of the follow-up appointment and with it came the silent car ride and the long-distance trek from the car to the waiting room. I expected the doctor to tell us it was all a terrible mistake, that the lab must have switched his results because they found millions of sperm. My heart was pounding when the doctor walked in the door. He had a little pep in his step, and I got excited.

"Have you all seen a geneticist yet?"

"No?" My husband and I answered in unison.

I followed up, "Why?"

"Well, we can't explain why your husband is not producing sperm. We believe he has what's called Azoospermia and possibly Hypogonadism. It's a condition where the male doesn't produce sperm due to the body not producing enough testosterone. Testosterone is also responsible for things such as muscle mass, strength, bone mass, sex drive, and even red blood cells.

"Maybe that's the reason why I haven't really gown facial hair?" My husband accepted.

"Could be," the doctor offered. "Did you have a medical condition when you were young?"

"No, not that I know of."

"Mumps?"

"I did, but my mom said she had them treated. I went to the doctor at the time and he didn't find anything wrong. I've never had any problems with my sex drive, well, until now. And, I work out and all of that so, I don't think that's an issue."

The doctor continued, "Did you have an accident to where you crushed your testicles?"

"I played football, but I never had someone crush my testicles." My husband winced at the thought.

"Do you feel weak or tired?" The doctor asked.

"I mean, sometimes I feel weak and tired, but I just thought it was because I was stressed and wasn't sleep well. Umm, I'm trying to think…"

"I'm surprised you're standing with your testosterone being so low."

My husband asked tentatively, "What do you mean my testosterone is low? How low is low?"

"Well, very low." The doctor stated, "The average for a man your age is about 300-1000 nanograms per deciliter. Yours is in the 50s."

"50's? Am I gonna die?"

I held my husband's hand.

"No, you are not going to die," the doctor relieved us, "but if we don't get you on some testosterone soon, it could lower your life expectancy. You can develop issues like osteoporosis, weight gain, loss of facial hair, fatigue, development of breast tissue, and your sex drive will continue to decrease."

"Well then, get him some testosterone," I quipped.

The doctor leaned back in his chair, "Well, see, there is no natural testosterone. Your husband will have to take synthetic testosterone. And, while it will make him better, I mean, 100 times better, it may make his chances of ever producing sperm non-existent, meaning that you may never be able to have a baby naturally. I say 'may' because I do believe in miracles. So, I will never say 'never.' There are some other medications we can try first to see if they will help spawn testosterone and sperm production. First, we will need to get a genetic test to see if there are chromosomal abnormalities that may be causing the issue. It could be a blockage, but with such low testosterone levels, we can't be sure."

My mind was racing. *Low life expectancy… never having a child naturally… I waited all this time to have you tell me you can't explain why this is happening? Isn't that your job?*

"Well, what does this mean?" I insisted. "You're giving us a lot of hypotheticals without explaining why this happened. For me, that's unacceptable. We're not paying for hypotheticals. We're paying for you to fix this."

I wanted to apologize to the doctor for my tone, but I felt like I deserved a pass given the news I just received. My husband and the doctor continued talking about testing and treatments. I saw their mouths move, but I could no longer hear the words. Terms I couldn't even spell were spilling out of the doctor's mouth. I wished he would stop talking, stop saying things I didn't understand, stop saying he didn't know why this was happening. He was supposed to tell us that my husband could simply take some pills and in six months we would be back up and running.

I excused myself from the room, claiming I had a phone call. I did not want to cry in front of my husband. I knew it would hurt his heart and make him angry, all at the same time. I stood in the bathroom staring in the mirror and the reflection of my tears. It was one thing to be told that he didn't have sperm. It was another thing not to know why. I didn't marry him for him to die on me sooner than we had planned. Synthetic testosterone? He needed it, but that would ruin our chances of ever being able to try to have a baby. I believed he would sacrifice himself for me, and at that moment, I was willing to let him do it for the sake of our baby. But, was that right? I was overwhelmed. I splashed my face with cold water, wiped it with a towel, and went back into the room.

The doctor said he wanted my husband to take a series of additional tests. He also needed to find out about his childhood, which meant my husband would have to tell his parents about the diagnosis.

"Your path to children may not be easy," the doctor paused before adding, "and may not happen at all. We are going to do what we can, but it's going to take time."

I knew he had said it before, but I wanted him to clarify, "What do you mean 'at all,' like never?"

"Well, as I mentioned before, with a condition like your husband's, couples usually don't produce children naturally. However, there are many ways you can still become parents with and without sperm."

I wanted to keep asking questions, hoping for a different response, but I knew it would be the same. No children from my husband. I may never be a mom. This was not what I signed up for. This was not why I paid insurance. The doctor was supposed to be able to fix this.

By the time we left the doctor's office, I needed a medical dictionary and encyclopedia to help me understand all that was said. To sum it up, having kids naturally was going to be impossible. But as the doctor said, "I don't have the final say. Let's just take it one day at a time."

I chose to live in denial, believing that in a few weeks, maybe six months, maybe a year, this would right itself and we'd have a baby. I wasn't ready for the possibility that the pain I felt could last forever. I didn't believe that we—the couple everyone expected to be parents by now—would not be able to have our own children.

A week before Christmas we got back the additional test results. Bottom line: my husband did not produce sperm, or testosterone for that matter. They found a piece of broken DNA but couldn't attribute it to a specific chromosome. If it had been a full XXY chromosome, then my husband would have had something called Klinefelter Syndrome (another term I knew nothing about, but that makes men sterile). However, it was not a full chromosome, and therefore, they had no further explanation. The doctor suggested putting my husband on a medication called Clomid to see if that would help increase his testosterone. He also talked about us exploring In Vitro Fertilization (IVF) and other means of having a child with help from a fertility specialist. However, IVF treatments were a minimum of $20,000—more than we could comfortably afford at that early stage in our careers. He mentioned adoption, but I wanted my own baby, not someone else's. I didn't even want him to mention sperm donation. I had already made up my mind that was not happening.

I was still holding out for God to perform a miracle the way he parted the Red Sea or turned water into wine. Certainly, he could make sperm out of nothing and increase my husband's testosterone.

Our parents had encouraged us to not give up on God because he hadn't given up on my husband and me. Truth is, I had given up months ago. The New Year arrived and, although we both began to slowly accept what the doctor told us, we decided to get a second opinion and see a new urologist. Or rather, *I* decided my husband should see a new urologist. He, of course, did not want to deal with it. I wanted him to see an expert, someone world-renowned on the subject of low testosterone. If there was a top doctor, I'm sure he or she could tell us that the issue could be fixed and that our other urologist was flat-out wrong. I did my research and found a leader in male infertility. He was booked for months, but I harassed his nurses until they found a way to squeeze my husband in for an appointment.

My poor husband went through the same process as the last doctor. But this specialist charged *more* money to tell us the exact same thing. "It could possibly be diagnosed as Klinefelter Syndrome, but you'll need to see a geneticist to confirm."

By May we had seen three different doctors. The geneticist hadn't been able to confirm if my husband had Klinefelter Syndrome. The Clomid was not working. My husband still was not producing sperm nor was his testosterone increasing. After not getting any new results with the new doctors, we began to feel like we were getting ripped off. We decided to go back to the first urologist. He again brought up synthetic testosterone, but since we were still holding on to hope of natural conception. He briefly mentioned the possibility of a testicular biopsy. It was a surgical procedure where the doctor would take a tissue sample from my husband's testicles to see if there was something blocking the sperm or to see if there were sperm in the testicles that did not show in the semen from the semen analysis. If they found sperm in the testicles he could retrieve it and use it for IVF. The doctor further explained that while he could move forward with the testicular biopsy, he felt like we weren't giving the Clomid time to work and he wasn't confident that he would find sperm when doing the surgery.

My husband flat out refused to have surgery on his most sensitive man parts. And I flat out refused to give up on having a child naturally. I was hell-bent on having a baby by the end of the year. Finding sperm in his testis would allow us to do IVF and we could have our baby. To me, the biopsy was the only answer. To my husband, surgery on his testicles was not even a question. He insisted that we just had to be patient.

"You are rushing it. It's not your problem, it's my problem. And it's my decision on what to do."

I wasn't listening. I wanted a baby. I wanted to be a mom. I deserved a baby and I was determined that his stubbornness was not going to keep it from me.

I knew his stubbornness was born of his fear about the surgery. I didn't yet realize that I was being stubborn too and it was also born of fear. I feared I would never be a parent. I feared that our parents would be too old to enjoy our kids if we did have them. I feared that I would have to accept that it was not God's will for us to have any children. Every time I thought about it, a knot swelled in my throat. I got headaches. Fear of the unknown kept me awake at night. I needed to know what the future held. I couldn't understand why no one could tell us how this all started. Why couldn't my husband produce sperm? All men have sperm. Why not him? It seemed like such a simple question deserving a simple answer. But it was more complex than I ever imagined.

CONFESSION: I was living under the assumption that everything had a clear answer. I expected that my husband's condition could be explained and summed up into a medical report that I could use to articulate to the world why we were childless. I held doctors in high regard, perhaps too high. I regarded them as all-knowing beings of the medical world. So, wasn't I surprised when no one could tell us what was wrong with my husband. Why did he, out of all the men in the world, have this rare condition, and why were we just finding out now? Through my faith, I began to understand that man was not made to know everything. And for us, knowing would not have changed our situation.

Truth 5: Infertile Females are Favorites

Semen Secret: Infertile women are the only ones that matter to the world. Infertile men are anomalies.

If the doctors couldn't give me the answer, surely the internet could. The world wide web was the source of all knowledge. However, the internet proved to be both a blessing and a curse. Every night my husband and I would spend hours researching his condition. There had to be somebody, somewhere, who had experienced what my husband and I were facing. But, every time I typed 'infertility' in an internet search, websites about infertile women popped up. There were support groups, financial offerings, blogs, TV shows, confessionals—all for women. Husbands of infertile women had all sorts of tools and resources they could use to help them and their wives get through the disappointment of being childless. But nowhere, not even in the Bible, was there mention of a *man* who had to deal with not being able to produce children. Nothing, nowhere.

I was furious at the lack of information and support for my situation. I began to loathe the women who talked about miscarriage. In my blind fury, I reasoned that at least they got to know what pregnancy felt like. They had experienced the excitement of reading a positive test. For a moment, they knew what it felt like to create life and have a baby inside of them. Some women felt a kick, others have a photograph from their ultrasound. I was too lost in my own pain to consider how deep their pain would have been to know that excitement, feel that life, and lose it all. I was too busy being jealous of their pregnancy to understand their loss. I was desperate to know what it was like to feel a child in my own belly. In hindsight, I wouldn't want their pain either.

With every Google search, my resentment for infertile women and their husbands grew. Where was the support group for my husband? Where were the books on how wives cope with infertile husbands? Where do *we* go? What do *we* do? How do *we* cope? I didn't want to be in a support group where everyone else was talking about the loss of their baby or their inability to get pregnant and I would be the only one in the room talking about my more than capable womb and his missing sperm. I had what they wanted, and they had what I wanted... there would always be a disconnect. What I realize now is that we all shared the pain of not being able to hold our own children in our arms. Like me, they would never know what a child who shared both of their features looked like. Their spouses probably had the same questions about their wives as I had about my husband. Yet, these were things I could not reconcile at the time because I was dealing with my own issues.

I looked at different studies on men with similar conditions as my husband and there were small but promising statistics that we could still conceive a child naturally if they did a more evasive testicular biopsy than the urologist had mentioned previously. This surgery would go deeper in the testis to search for sperm. Side effects included a longer recovery and worse scarring. I wanted him to try it, but I knew the surgery discussion would bring about arguments. He would say, *your body is not the one that is messed up. I'm the one that's sick.* I was sick of hearing that. It was my struggle too. I felt like he was being selfish to tell me I couldn't feel a certain way about not being able to have a child.

I had had enough. My internet research had both infuriated and empowered me. I got up from my computer and walked downstairs. My husband was sitting on the couch watching TV and talking on the phone to one of his friends. I politely tapped him on the shoulder and told him we needed to talk. In my mind, I was going to tell him about all the infertile women and the way they were relentless in their pursuit to have a child. I was going to let him know that he needed to be relentless too. I guess he could sense that I wanted to talk about the baby because he paused to look up from the phone at me, only to turn back around to keep talking.

What I had to say was important. He could ignore me for as long as he wanted but I was going to get through to him. I could feel myself getting angry by the minute. The rehearsed words began to get jumbled in my head. My bold stance ended in disaster. By the time he got off the phone, I was crying.

Through the tears, I screamed, "I'm never gonna know what it's like to be a mom! Never!"

I mentioned the surgery and he yelled back at me, "You are always making this about you. It's my body. I am the one with the problem! Me!"

He was right, it was his body, but it was *my* baby, and he was the holdup. I felt bad for blaming him, but I was fuming. The testicular biopsy would help us determine if there was even a chance that we could have a baby of our own.

That night we slept in separate rooms, me alone with my tears, and him alone with his pain. My head hurt from trying to think of the things we must have done to bring this situation on us. I had nothing. I went from blaming God, to blaming his parents, to blaming the doctors, to blaming him, to blaming myself for not asking more questions.

I kept going over in my mind if I would have married him if he would have told me he couldn't have children. The holier than thou part of me said *yes, I love you, not your sperm*. That wasn't true though. It would probably have declined the ring. I wanted to be a mommy. If we didn't make it through this, my first date question would be, *Nevermind about your job or any psychological issues, do you have sperm?*

We didn't speak for a week. It was miserable because we were friends and I had always been able to share my thoughts with him. But, I was too prideful. He was keeping me from my dream. I was so confident they would find sperm with the biopsy that I couldn't understand why he wouldn't just have the stupid surgery. We could get the sperm, do IVF, and save some sperm for later. It seemed so simple to me.

By that autumn, we had seen at least five doctors who had diagnosed and re-diagnosed my husband, and the arguments began to swell like a tsunami. The wave was rushing towards our shore, threatening to destroy our once perfect marriage. I searched for blogs on male infertility. Of the few that were available, I read stories of women leaving their husbands when they found out. Or, on the flip side, I found infertile women who got so wrapped up in their conditions that their husbands decided to pack up and leave. I could identify with both scenarios.

CONFESSION: I hate the fact that society sees infertility as a woman's issue. The world would have us believe that men don't have problems making babies. Society paints a picture where it is the woman saying, *I'm sorry*, and drowning in her sorrow because she can't give her husband his namesake. The inverse of this is the anomaly. My husband's infertility was like sighting Bigfoot. There was *nothing* out there to help women like me deal with a husband who was unable to make sperm, and very little to help the man cope with his personal infertility struggle.

Truth 6: Modern Medicine Isn't Magic

Semen Secret: A little doctor visit here, a little surgery there, sprinkle a little medicine on top and Voila!... Your infertility is instantly cured!

As I read more articles, it seemed that the only way for us to attempt pregnancy would be through invitro. I made an appointment to go to an information session to find out about IVF. They wanted couples to come together, but my husband was insistent that he was not going with me. After a few arguments and a lot of tears, he reluctantly agreed to go. The urologist had already warned us that the cost of the procedure was $20,000 at minimum, but we didn't realize that was the cost for only for one cycle. If I didn't get pregnant the first time, we would have to pay for additional cycles. One couple had done three cycles before they were successful.

Why should we have to pay so much for something that was supposed to come so naturally? The doctors at the informational suggested we could finance the IVF procedure. They provided testimonials and statistics about how many successful trials they had completed, but we knew it was a gamble. $20,000 just to try and have a baby? At that price, we wanted a guarantee. And money was the least of our problems because, without the surgery to collect the sperm, IVF wasn't even an option for us. The surgery was the only way I could get pregnant with my husband's child, but he adamantly refused to consider the option. And he thought I was selfish.

The next week, for some stupid reason, we decided to have a Labor Day party at the house. It should have been called the "Fake It" party. The type of party where you fake like you like each other but it's probably the first time in weeks you've talked to each other. If you're lucky, it'll be a "Fake It till You Make It" party and after pretending to like each other you may actually make up. When the guests arrived, questions about babies arrived with them, and the fake smile accompanied by the "We're waiting on God" comments came soon after. I wished that people would stay out of my womb. The party couldn't end soon enough and when it was over we did not make up. It made me sick to have to say two words to my husband. He was blocking my baby, and I was getting on his nerves. There was nothing for us to discuss.

That next week, a few days before our anniversary, my husband sent me a text:

> I'll have the surgery.

I couldn't believe it! I took a screenshot, printed it, and tucked it away because I wanted proof in case he tried to back out. It took all my willpower, but I was patient and waited until he brought it up when he got home. I didn't want my questions to push him away. That same day we made an appointment with the doctor to get the details about the surgery. I was thrilled. My babies were getting closer. I even repented for my evil thoughts about my husband on Labor Day.

The surgery was scheduled for the week before Christmas. Leading up to the surgery, my husband went in for blood work and testing to prep for surgery. Every day I prayed and thanked the Lord for my husband's ability to make sperm and testosterone. I prayed with my prayer partner at work. I wrote down scriptures that I repeated every night. Psalm 84:11 and God not withholding any good thing, Deuteronomy 7:14 and no one among us being barren, Psalms 103:3 and how God heals sickness and disease, and even Psalms 139:13-17 about God forming us. I was speaking faith, naming and claiming my breakthrough.

I assumed that our health insurance would cover the procedure. I thought insurance covered everything. My husband was sick, and having a baby was necessary. However, we found out our insurance, and most insurance companies only covered the diagnosis of male infertility. Treatments could only be used to increase testosterone levels, but not for conception. Thus, every time we went to an office visit for infertility, we would have to pay an upfront cost and then see if our insurance would cover the payment. I spent hours on the phone arguing about the need for coverage, and it was frustrating. Infertility was a sickness, so why wouldn't the insurance companies cover it? The constant out-of-pocket expense frustrated my husband, but I kept trying to assure him I was going to do whatever it took to get the insurance to cover some of the cost. I knew that if I didn't show him my persistence, he might back out of the surgery and I would lose any chance of having a baby.

The day of the surgery had finally come! I was so excited about the surgery, finding sperm, and getting on to our next chapter as parents. My husband's parents came to help with the recovery. My husband was nervous, but I was calm—I had prayed and fasted. I knew that the sperm was hiding and we would find them in a few hours. Then it would be my turn to have surgery, the IVF procedure.

The Bible says that 'he is healed,' so I knew my husband had sperm waiting for us to find them. I trusted God would not take away our dream of having a baby. We would be fruitful and multiply, replenish the Earth. God had been testing us to see if we would trust Him. *You are so funny God*, I thought. His Word would not come back void and I would get my baby, even if it was created in a Petri dish! There was no way God would bring us to this point and not give us the child we deserved.

After a brief prayer from his dad, my husband was wheeled to surgery. The three-hour procedure seemed like an eternity. But I was excited. I daydreamed about IVF and getting pregnant. I wanted to insert three fertilized eggs, just in case one or two didn't make it.

My daydreams were interrupted with the when the doctor finally entered the waiting room. My heart was pounding, but I was smiling. I wanted to know how many sperm he had found.

"Well, we did the surgery… and we didn't find any sperm."

I slumped down in my chair. "I fasted, I prayed, I believed! Why? Why would God do this to us?" These words I thought I was saying in my mind were spewing out so loudly that my mother-in-law came to sit beside me and hold my hand.

"I'm here with you," she assured me, "I'm here."

I pleaded with the doctor, "There has to be some mistake. You have to look again! Please, look again! There must be something there. This was supposed to work!"

My mother-in-law asked the technical questions only a nurse would know to ask. My father-in-law left the room. I was sure he didn't want me to see him cry.

My face burned from the saltwater tears that were streaming down my face and pooling into the couch. I was crying so uncontrollably that I began to feel dizzy. *Pull it together,* I kept telling myself. However, I couldn't function. I remember a nurse helping me to the bathroom so I could get myself together. I couldn't let my husband see me in that state.

Up until the surgery, I believed that my husband could produce sperm and that the heartache we had endured would be temporary. I couldn't allow myself to believe that God would make me a childless wife. Although I wanted a baby, it was my husband that had to believe it could happen for us, that he could be healed. Maybe it was his lack of faith that caused the surgery to fail.

I heard the nurse saying, "It will be okay. You can still be parents. There are so many other ways to do this."

JUST SHUT UP! I wanted to scream. I needed her to stop talking to me. It was not okay. I managed to politely ask the nurse to leave me alone for a few moments. I needed to be alone with my thought.

I didn't have the stamina to call my parents, so I sent them a text:

> It didn't work. There is no sperm. NOTHING! Please DO NOT come here. I just don't want to talk about it.

When I finally gathered myself together, I went to the patient recovery room. My husband's parents insisted that I go back to see my husband alone. I walked to his bedside smiling.

"I know you've been crying. They told me they didn't find anything. I'm sorry. It's my fault you can never have kids."

"But you're wrong," I said, "I don't view this as your fault. You didn't make you."

Though, even if he didn't admit it, I knew he had hoped that there would be some sperm. Finding sperm and being able to produce children was his opportunity to redeem his "manhood"—to feel normal again. I had no doubt he was crushed by the finding. I tried to comfort and reassure him as best as I could, but I knew he didn't believe me. We had known each other since we were kids. He knew I was devastated. As a man, he was supposed to fix things and protect me. I could tell in his eyes that he felt like a failure, that there was nothing he could do to protect me from the pain I was feeling. In my attempt to make him feel like I wasn't bothered, I asked what was next, ready to make a plan for adoption or another treatment. In hindsight, the question was too soon, too insensitive.

"That's all you are worried about," my husband fumed. "I just cut my balls open! I'm not thinking about anything else!"

I realized struck a nerve and I tried to calm him down, but I had gone too far. I was desperate to find a solution to this problem and the words came out of my mouth before I knew what I was saying. He wanted a child just as bad or even more than me. He was broken, mentally, physically, and emotionally. But all I could think about was my disappointment. I did care about him and his health, but at that time I cared about having a baby a little bit more. Being a mommy had become my first priority and being a wife was running a close second.

To add injury to insult, my husband's younger sister was having a baby, and it was going to be a boy.

The one thing he wanted was to carry on his father's name.

He was defeated, "I guess I will never have a boy to carry on our name."

There was nothing I could do to fix that feeling for him. I felt like it was so unfair. Why was it that time and time again everyone around us was able to so effortlessly produce the one thing that for us seemed impossible? I wasn't sure where to put those feelings. I had cried, I had been angry, and at times, I had even been rude to people who were having babies. It wasn't because I wasn't happy for them—I was, but it was supposed to be me. I wondered how they deserved a baby, and I didn't. Every time I turned on the TV someone had abandoned, hurt, or put their baby up for adoption. I could not understand how a God would give a person a baby they didn't want but leave people like my husband and I wondering what was wrong with us.

I tried to make the days of recovery light-hearted. I knew for him it was painful, both the surgery and the fact that it was not successful. I wanted him to open up about how he felt about it all, but I knew he was not going to tell me anything. I tried to stand in the gap for him emotionally the best way I knew how. I politely asked all visitors not to talk about having a baby or even ask me how I felt. I definitely didn't want it mentioned to my husband. We had been together long enough to know how to read our unspoken queues, those eye movements to let the other know that you were not okay and that you didn't want to be bothered.

I finally decided to call my parents. There were few words, lots of tears. They dropped everything to visit for the weekend. Before they walked in I asked them not to mention anything about the surgery or babies. I wasn't ready, but my dad didn't listen, "I know that this is hard for you, but sometimes we have to deal with things we don't understand. I want you to know that we don't care how you have a baby or if you have a baby. We love you both just the same. Whatever you all want to do, whatever you decide, no matter how much it costs or what it takes, we will do it to see you both happy."

His words were heartfelt. He wanted to reassure me that he would try to fix it for me. They stayed for the weekend. The night before they left, my mom emailed my husband and I a scripture: Mark 11:23-24 *Truly I say to you, whoever says to this mountain, 'Be taken up and cast into the sea,' and does not doubt in his heart, but believes that what he says is going to happen, it will be granted him. Therefore, I say to you, all things for which you pray and ask, believe that you have received them, and they will be granted you.*

In true mom fashion, the words went unspoken as I had requested. She reminded me that while I made it clear she could not *say* anything, I didn't say she couldn't *do* something. I rolled my eyes and smiled.

Their presence took my mind off the obvious. When everyone had gone back home, we were in the house alone, waiting on the New Year and hopefully a new beginning. At least we knew that, for the time being, having a baby naturally was over. That chapter was closed, and though I desperately wanted to open the book again and rewrite the story, it was beyond my control.

After the failed surgery, my husband and I drifted back into our siloed depression where we barely spoke to each other, avoided our friends, and pretended our world wasn't collapsing around us. Then one day, while doing my incessant research, I came across an article that discussed a medication, Human Chorionic Gonadotropin (HCG). It was prescribed to women, but men could also take it in hopes that it would boost testosterone levels, thereby boosting sperm count.

At my husband's follow-up appointment, I mentioned HCG to the urologist. To my frustration, the doctor had never prescribed HCG to his patients. "I'll have to research it and get back to you." Of course, my impatience was demanding that he take a few hours—Google it and get back to us ASAP. But I had to give him a week.

A week later, he told us that he would prescribe HCG on a trial basis for six months. I was all smiles again, certain that this was the answer. The only drawback was the tiny vial of precious medicine was over $150 each month. To make it even worse, our insurance was adamant that they were not covering the medication. *Are you freaking kidding me?*

For three months we were in a WWF Smackdown fight with the insurance company to get them to determine that HCG was a medical necessity.

Eventually, they agreed to a minimal reduction in the cost of the medication, and we could focus on the process of administering the treatment. The medication was an injectable that had to be given at the same time every day. My husband didn't like shots and I had to play nurse. That was a disaster. We argued every time I would get ready to give him the shot because I was timid with the needle and he was ready to get it over with. Some days we went to bed and forgot to administer the medication. Sadly, what started out as a way to fix our problems, turned into one more reason for us to argue and shout.

The medication was a source of tension. It had become the kryptonite to our marriage and communication. After three months of taking the medication, my husband broke down and declared, "I'm just not paying for that shit anymore! It's too expensive. I'm not giving myself shots for the rest of my life."

My husband's stubbornness that so often stifled our plans was back in full force. We needed six months to see if the medication was going to work. It had only been three months. I slammed the needle down on the counter and stormed off to my car. I didn't drive away, I just sat parked in my driveway, crying and listening to the radio.

I let the music flow through my veins. I listened to love songs, worship songs, sad songs, happy songs, even songs that made me laugh about me and my husband. It was at that moment I was reminded that maybe I was where I was supposed to be. The music told a story that led me to a small sense of acceptance. After a few hours, I gathered all my snotty tissues and headed back into the house. I sat in the shower until I felt like I had washed away all the sadness from that evening. For the first time in a long time, I slept soundly, and I slept close to my husband.

CONFESSION: I believed that the medical interventions were going to work. I prayed, I believed, I trusted that God would give me the desires of my heart. What I wasn't prepared for was when God said NO. This was on His time, not mine. I again found myself grieving over our unmet expectations. I expected surgery to be my miracle. I expected the medicine to be magic. I expected there to be sperm. I assumed God was going to heal my husband. I was not sure how to process what I thought was an unanswered prayer. My devastation coupled with my husband's disappointment was more than I felt I could bear. I could not see God in anything that was happening. I had been taught that science and God were supposed to complement each other. Yet, the science had failed and so did my prayers. I never considered the fact that there were no guarantees they would work. That was a hard lesson to learn.

Truth 7: "Just Adopt"

Semen Secret: Adoption is the cure for infertility. It's so easy!

Since natural birth, IVF, and the experimental medication had all been eliminated as options, we reluctantly decided to investigate adoption. We scanned adoption websites. Looking at the pictures of little babies cheered us up and I was relieved to finally be moving in a direction towards parenthood. Private adoptions were expensive, so we hoped that going through the state would cut down on cost. We agreed we wanted children three years old or younger. We registered for an adoption orientation with Department of Family and Children Services to learn more about the process.

I was getting excited.

About a week before orientation, I showed my husband a baby boy on the website who was available for adoption.

"Maybe we could ask about him during orientation," I mused.

"I don't want a boy."

I wanted to yell, *Are you freakin' kidding me right now? Beggars can be choosers and you are putting a stipulation on something you can't even have on your own?*

Instead, I said, "I want a baby. As long as it's healthy, that's what I want. Boy or girl."

"You better be glad I'm even considering this. It is my issue and I'm not giving another boy my last name who is not biologically mine," he retorted.

I did my usual, ran to my room to cry. He did his usual, sat with a screwed-up face for a few days.

By the day of the adoption meeting, we were both a little eager and nervous. The room was packed with people who wanted to be parents. The first part of the meeting discussed foster care. For us, foster care wasn't an option because we wanted a child to raise as our own, but the goal of foster care is to "reunite children with their biological parents." My husband and I disagreed on many things, but we both agreed that once we had a baby in our home, we did not want to give it back, especially to a parent who had the child taken away in the first place.

I sent him a text:

> I'm not giving a baby back to someone who abused it.

He responded:

> Yeah we're not doing that.

When the adoption portion of the orientation came up, we stopped texting to pay attention. The facilitator ran down all the benefits of adopting through the state. They warned that we may have to take siblings, but we were okay with two children as long as they met our age requirement. It seemed all good until the last slide:

"The waiting list to adopt an infant is three years long."

Three years? And still, there was no guarantee? We both rolled our eyes. Another roadblock. We left the orientation with our hopes dashed again.

Even with the three-year wait, we decided to apply for a home study to start the process. That proved to be a mistake. The home study was a degrading interrogation. The social worker asked questions that felt intimate and insulting, and then she still had to walk through to our home to see if it was suitable for a child.

She went from one room to the next critiquing every nook and cranny in our home.

"You are going to need double-sided locks on all of these doors and childproof locks on the cabinet in the bathroom. Otherwise, when we come to visit, you could be reprimanded. You also will need locks on your gates and you will need to do a fire drill where you can get all doors unlocked and the baby out in under three minutes."

I interrupted, "Are you serious?"

She replied, "Yes, unfortunately, I am. These are the state rules if you want to get a child in your home. I don't make them. I just have to follow them."

The more she spat out rules, the more we were ready for her to go. We didn't need her judgment. We would be awesome parents. If only God would give us a baby. By the time she left, we knew that state adoption was a no-go.

Our next move was to look at a private adoption center where we would establish a relationship with a pregnant mother who wanted to find adoptive parents before the child was born. The price quotes seemed like a game of the Price Is Right: $20,000, $40,000, $60,000, to include the fees for Uber rides for the mom to get back and forth from the doctor. Opposite of the website where we looked at children for adoption, this service had a site where moms could view us, the "prospective parents." It was a lot to absorb and neither my husband nor I were ready for the process.

While I was spending my time looking for adoption agencies, my husband was letting himself go and complaining all the damn time. I was sick of his complaining. He knew he had to be in good health if he hoped to increase his testosterone and give his sperm a chance to grow, but he wasn't doing that. He was the reason why I was combing over adoption sites. I felt like he was being lazy on purpose. He kept saying "you don't care about me. You only want this baby." He was right, to a point. I cared, but just so that I could have what I wanted. I wanted a child. My age 30 deadline had come and gone. My biological clock was ticking. Adoption, sperm donation, invitro... what I wanted was to miss my period, get a positive pregnancy test, and have my husband's child.

CONFESSION: You cannot "just adopt." Adoption is not a simple process. Although there are millions of kids out there who need a loving home, the system is so convoluted that it takes an act of God to get a child. The process is set up to ensure people who don't have a child's best interest in mind can't get a child, but it also makes it difficult for loving parents to adopt. From the enormous amount of paperwork, to the money, to the home visit, a couple could spend more than $20,000 and wait up to 18 months before they ever hold a baby in their arms. Or, even worse, the biological parent can decide at the last moment to keep the child, crushing the adoptive parent's dreams and negate the money, time, and effort spent on the process. Adoption is a risk and each couple needs to spend time deciding if it's the right risk for their relationship.

Truth 8: Baby Showers Bring Storms

Semen Secret: When bad things happen, you have to suck it up and accept it. You have to be happy for others. When you celebrate with others, you feel better.

Another New Year was approaching, and I was hoping it would bring new beginnings for us. I tried to convince myself that I was going to be okay with only being a party of two. I convinced myself I was fine. I even got invited to my first baby shower since my husband's surgery. I was ready to face my nemesis: other pregnant women. I walked into Baby's-R-Us for the first time in about a year. I was determined I was going in the store—no online shopping for me.

The store was full of pregnant women and people with their newborns. I stood in line waiting to access the registry kiosk. As I looked around the store at happy mothers, I realized I was less prepared for this emotional test that I had imagined. The two women in front of me were trying to determine what was left to purchase on their registries. Though the wait was only a few minutes, it seemed liked hours. I felt like the world was punishing me. I just wanted to get this damn registry gift and get out of the store. The printed registry sheets couldn't come out of the kiosk fast enough.

As I walked down each aisle, I saw happy parents with their babies. Husbands and wives were scanning items. Big pregnant stomachs made it difficult for me to maneuver around the store. I held up fine until I got to the clothing section. I was surrounded by adorable pink and blue onesies and bonnets and booties and it hit me that I may never be able to shop for my own baby. Before I knew it, I was crying.

An older woman with her daughter walked by and placed a hand on my shoulder, "I know how you feel. My daughter got overwhelmed when we went to pick out clothes for her new baby. Just let the tears of happiness flow!

Semen Secrets

Congratulations. When is your due date?"

I was so choked up I couldn't respond. I offered the woman a weak smile and ran out of the store. The car seemed so far away, but if I could just reach it I could let my tears flow without anyone looking.

I was defeated. I couldn't go into another Baby's-R-Us, Baby Depot, Toys-R-Us, or even the baby section in a Target or Wal-Mart. If it involved babies, I just wasn't strong enough to handle it. I went back to shopping online.

Baby showers brought me storms of emotions—from sadness, to anger, to jealously, to defeat. The showers forced me to visit places, both physically and emotionally, where I didn't have the strength to go. They reminded me of what I couldn't have, what we couldn't be: parents.

I felt like an idiot. I hadn't expected something so trivial to affect me so severely. The shower invitations came as constant reminders of my empty womb. I started putting all the invites in a box. I never went to any of the showers. When people would call for my RSVP, I would make up stories: "I have a work trip." "We're going out of town." "Girl, I'm not feeling well." All the while, I was sitting at home seething at the fact that I was always a guest but may never be the one having the shower. I would mail a gift and add a cheesy note: "Congrats on your Blessing! Can't wait to meet your bundle of joy!" I was lying. I didn't want to meet their bundle of joy a.k.a. reminder of my sorrow. I wasn't happy for them. I didn't know how to be happy for the person who had everything I wanted.

I stopped looking at social media. Scrolling through the endless pictures of fat bellies and baby reveals made me cringe. It seemed like everybody in the world was able to experience the joys of expectant parenthood except us. Sometimes I would scroll through Pinterest and daydream about what baby shower theme I would have, who I would invite, and what my games would be. I would walk to the room in our house that I wanted to be the nursey and sit in a daze trying to visualize where I would put the crib, toys, and my rocking chair.

CONFESSION: I tried to force myself to be in a place of acceptance too fast. I was sick of pretending to be happy for others when I was hurting so deeply. I had to be honest with myself that I wasn't ready to deal with another person's happiness. I thought that going to these baby showers would show how strong I was, show the world I was unbothered. But, what I really needed to do was give myself time. I needed time to heal. Faking it until I had my own baby was going to get old and no one needed my sour attitude at an event that was meant to celebrate something as joyous as a baby. It was okay if I didn't go, and I didn't have to explain why. If I didn't allow myself to feel the pain, I could never get over my emotions.

Truth 9: Husband Hatred Happens

Semen Secret: Thou shall not hate; especially not your husband.

Christmas again. We were still subjected to be happy and buy gifts for kids who were not our own. The holidays were miserable for us. Christmas was for children—which we didn't have. Christmas was to celebrate a birth—something we had never experienced. The holidays were about spending time with the one you loved—yet I couldn't stand when my husband walked in a room, and I know he felt the same about me. We shared a few smiles and occasional happy moments, but the anger and resentment far outweighed the good. I was depressed, although I didn't realize it then. I was merely going through the motions. Wake up, go to work, smile, run errands, smile, take care of home, go to bed. I hated my life. More than that, I hated my husband.

Everything, big and small was the source of an argument. *You didn't put the dishes up the right way. Why did you park the car in the middle of the driveway? You left the lights on. I don't like how you folded my shirts. You're talking too loud. Turn down the TV. Stop snoring.*

I couldn't stand to be in the same room with him and I let him know it. He was equally rude and nasty. I was the source of his pain and he was the object of my sorrow. Every day it was the same conversation.

Him: "Hey"

Me: "Hey"

Two words and we would go our separate ways. I would watch TV in the basement. He would watch TV upstairs. We would get on the phone and talk to anyone so we wouldn't have to talk to each other.

I imagined my life if I had chosen another man to be my husband. I mean, there were so many others I could have chosen from. Well, maybe not, but I imagined that I had a wide selection. I'm sure they had sperm. I could be happy right now with our kids. We would also be having sex every single day. My husband rarely touched me, and I couldn't help but take it personally. Then again, I didn't want to be touched at the time. When we did have sex, we just went through the motions, pretending to like it. I believed some days he was faking it, and so was I. What was once so enjoyable became a chore.

We tried to go out with our friends. Maybe being around other couples would make me like my husband better and him like me. Nope. Other people just made us realize how much we got on each other's nerves, especially when the other couples gushed over their kids.

I was overwhelmed by the idea of trying to stay positive. How could I deal with my husband and this condition for the rest of my life? Each temper tantrum made me reconsider divorce. Maybe he would be happier if he was alone to deal with his issue. Maybe I would be happier if I moved on and had a baby. I'm ashamed to admit that what kept me from breaking my vows was not the fact that divorce should never be an option, but the fact that I didn't want to be the bad guy. I didn't want my husband to be able to say, "She left me. I didn't leave her." Or for others to say, "Did you hear why she divorced him? Well, I heard…" I was too prideful to deal with the whispers and defend myself.

My husband would taunt me, "You can go ahead and leave. Go ahead, I'll be fine. That's what you wanna do anyway. I'm not keeping you here. I know this baby is more important to you me. I told you from the jump I didn't think you could live with me like this. That's why I told you to leave in the first place!"

I would reply, "You can leave if you feel like someone else would make you happy. I'm obviously not what you want. You want someone else. You always make this about you then say I'm making it about me. I won't give you the satisfaction of divorce."

A divorce would let people know we were having problems, and neither of us wanted that. We still couldn't talk about the problem openly, let alone talk about infertility and divorce.

I blamed him for the fact that I went through all these emotions. I could feel myself beginning to hate him and he hate me. He kept me from my dream and I was a constant reminder that he couldn't offer me my dream.

At some point I thought, *if a baby can cause this much drama, maybe we don't need a kid*. But, on the other hand, I wasn't a quitter. I had been fighting for this baby years, and I would continue to fight.

Month after month, period after period, I grew more discouraged. I hoped for a miracle—that one day my period would be late and my belly would swell with a little one. I felt selfish and yet I couldn't control my grief. On our anniversary, I sunk even lower into to my despair because I couldn't escape the thought that a baby may never happen for me... for us. I desperately wanted to be a mommy, to feel what it was like to have a life inside of me. I wanted my husband to be a father. I wanted our parents to be alive and well to share in the experience. But it seemed like it was never going to be. No matter how hard I prayed, my husband's testosterone still didn't increase, we still didn't have a baby and, to top it off, we were falling out of love with one another.

CONFESSION: It's okay to be angry at your spouse. Anger is a natural emotion, but hate is something completely different. Hate comes out of a rage that should never manifest itself. However, for me, it did. It's amazing how people forget to love when they need that love the most. I realized that when people say, "for better or worse," they only want to focus on the better because when the worst comes, they may not know how to deal with it. My hate was born of my desire for a baby. I made my husband the object of my anger, the source of my pain. Even if it's unintentional, we all look for scapegoats to try to project our innermost hurts. I felt inadequate and I feared the world would judge me for not being a mom more harshly than it judged him for not being a father. I hated him because he couldn't fill the void created by my inadequacy. I realize, now, he was never meant to fill that void in the first place.

Truth 10: Admit Anger at God

Semen Secret: You must love God with everything you have. You cannot hate the One that gave you life. I mean, he's God!

I was sick of hearing people tell me to pray and trust that God would change our situation. I even let my mom convince me to pick the room in our house where we wanted our nursery to be and buy baby clothes. I felt so stupid. Those clothes and that room were constant reminders of what I didn't have.

My husband and I were a couple of faith, but my faith failed me in this ordeal every time. If God was a good God, He would not allow us to suffer in this way. And, where was Jesus? He turned water into wine, healed the sick, and raised the dead with one touch of his hand. But where was Jesus when I needed him? He could change my situation in an instant. He could change my husband. Or could He?

There was no new equation. By God's math, $1+1=0$. That's how many children I had. Zero. That's how many sperm my husband had. Zero. That's how much love I still had for my husband. Zero. By the end of the year, that summed up my faith as well. Zero.

I had always journaled to God about everything and even though He wasn't fixing my situation, I still wrote to him like he was my best friend. A best friend who had disappointed and angered me, but a friend none the less. As another year rolled in, my tears ran on the pages of my journal, smearing the ink and blurring my vision. My T-shirt was wet with my tears. I was hot from crying and my mouth was dry. My head was ringing and my heart was racing. I was circling through the Stages of Grief again. I was bargaining and blaming. I searched for the God who had always been with me and I couldn't find Him anywhere. Our parents had always taught us to believe "God can do anything." I began to think that they lied to us. I couldn't wrap my mind around all those miracles I read about in the Bible and accept that he couldn't give my husband one sperm and a healthy baby. I wasn't asking him to part the Red Sea. He gave people babies every day. How could such a good God be so cruel to us?

I went back through my journal, hoping to discover some solace in the entries but page after page reminded me of how much I was angry with God.

November 5

Dear God, yesterday I got some news that made my heart stop. He ~~can't~~ *did not produce sperm. No to mention, he has completely shut down. My heart grieves for him because I think he thinks he failed me... he failed us. You have these dreams of what you think your life will be like. You worry and stress over silly things and then what matters hits you in your face. You realize that though you want a promotion, you want children even more. And though adoption is an option, I am sure there is no feeling like a kick or a hand pressing your stomach, to see and hear a heartbeat of someone else in your own body... to know that's what you made. To see what you both look like. I desperately want to be pregnant with TJ and Peyten. I do understand James 1:12 that I have to persevere under trial. But, my concern is for him. Is my faith strong enough to pull us both through? I don't know if I'm strong enough. I am writing this vision and making it plain because I will be able to conceive & he will be able to produce. Romans 4:17 says You give life to the dead. In Isaiah 43:2 You are with us in deep waters. 1 Peter 1:6-7, my faith is just being tested. I WILL NOT question You God, I won't. Just as You healed in Mark 5;334, You can do the same for me. I pray for a sound mind for us both. We are saved by faith (Ephesians 2:8), protected by faith (1 Peter 1:5) and have victory by faith (1 John 5:45). I don't have the spirit of fear for my family and I pray Psalm 91 over them. So, God, I still believe it will happen & I thank You for good reports and finances to do whatever we have to have these babies. But, I pray for my husband. He hurts, so I hurt too. Please help me help him. I can do nothing at this point but totally and completely lean on You. Help God. Be faithful to us! You will never withhold any good thing from us and children are a good thing. I just need You...*

I don't know what else to say... Amen.

November 23

Lord, I come to You with a clear heart and believe that You will do what You promised for us. You know our deep desire to conceive a child together. But, first, please heal my husband's heart, his feeling of being inadequate. Please help him become un-hurt, un-angry, un-sad. That is something only You can do. I rebuke the devil and I bind any ~~problem~~ infertility and extra chromosomes and risk factors associated with that and any disease the devil tries to inflict on my husband. As his heart grieves, bless me and give me the strength to be strong for him. Help me to help him. Devil, you will not steal my husband and children away from me. We will have a long life together and will have a family. I will carry my children in my womb from his sperm. We will have two healthy babies and our parents will be granted long, extended lives so our children can get to physically know them and our whole family. Please bless whatever option we have to go through to have these children... I will not accept that my husband is infertile. Show Yourself to the world. Show Yourself to my husband. I thank You that TJ and Peyten will be healthy and strong and that we will get to see their children and their children's children... I will just have to lean on You and never doubt.

December 6

Why am I so upset? Because now, I really want a baby. My mind swirls. I want our parents to be in good health. I want my husband to be in good health! We are supposed to grow old together! I want my kids to see all of this. It's just something I want really bad. And God, I still believe You can do it. ~~But when You see fit?~~ But I guess it will be when You see fit. I just have to go on Your promise and know that Your word will not come back void. You didn't bring us here to leave us. I still believe we can get pregnant through normal intercourse. I ask You to bless the doctor. Bless us financially, to pay for these doctor visits. Help my husband in his sadness. Thank You for showing him that in Your eyes, he is normal.

You made him perfect, in Your own image, and You have a son...

January 6

Dear God, I am seeking You to do a work in me. I enter into this New Year with fasting and prayer, it was only right that Fasting + Prayer + Faith = the ANSWER TO MY PRAYERS! Seems easy enough. In fact, I have a list of things that should manifest in 21 days:

1. My husband's healing

2. My healing

3. Financial Freedom

4. Family health, strength, longevity

5. TJ & Peyten

6. Understanding my purpose

7. Healthy marriage

8. Healthy body

9. More commitment

February 11

Does this mean You are not going to give us a baby? I mean, it did say that no doesn't last forever, but are You saying no, like no, or no like, not right now, or no like not today? How do I go on? How do I deal?

I don't understand? I don't want to be disobedient. I look at what I have and realize I have more than most. I know it could be worse and that I shouldn't compare to other people, but, am I allowed to be sad and disappointed? I want my own baby! I want to experience being a mom. I want to know what my husband and I look like when You combine our DNA. I want to know that! ~~It CANNOT be NO!~~ *Well, it can be no, but I thank You that my husband's sperm will increase, we will have these children. I know You just mean NO like to teach me a lesson or something. I guess...*

March 3

I just believe that my husband will produce sperm. That all this will soon be a memory. I want this for everyone and me. Everyone wants a baby. Just PLEASE do what You promised! IT's hard being happy for everyone else when you want a baby, your husband is the problem, and he is so negative. It's really hard to keep up on the inside. I believe God, Just help me to stay strong. I just want to thank You in advance for this.

May 30

REALLY GOD? IS THIS REALLY WHAT YOU WANT? DO YOU SEE THIS? MAYBE HE IS NOT THE ONE FOR ME?

July 19

I feel defeated. I'm not sure how much more I can be broken. My heart hurts and my tears burn my face. I have a bruise under my nose from where I have wiped it so much. And I'm trying not to blame him for his anger. I know he is hurting too, and that hurt people hurt people. But, where do hurt people go when they are in the same place and they need each other? I cannot do this alone. A baby. That's all we are asking for... a baby. You give them out every day. I'm just not sure why You have decided to skip my home. I just don't know how I'm going to do this. I just feel like giving up.

August 4

Dear God, I know You will redeem the time. To make it as if time was never lost. I will never stop believing that You will give me children. Our own fruit. I just have to believe my husband will produce sperm and that this pain I am in will go away. Just PLEASE, DO WHAT YOU PROMISED! It's hard being happy for everyone else when you want a baby and your spouse is so negative. It's hard to keep up on the inside. I believe God. Just help me to be strong.

September 8

As I approach my 7th anniversary, I just want to say Thank You. To hear her say (You know, who does my nails and wax) say that I have a good man is awesome. Of course, I know we will be great parents despite our current reality and I just believe that TJ and Peyten will be born of my husband's sperm. I look forward to carrying our children. I know our parents will be well able to enjoy them as well. And I want my husband and I to enjoy them, our children, and our children's children. I also thank You for our careers and our life right now as husband and wife. But, I wish I could see the future. I wish I could see what You see. I want to see a glimpse of my children. Just to know, to have some type of affirmation that they are still going to be. Just give me a sign. Something. I need something.

November 27

Okay so do You not see me again?!?!? Do You not see us?!?!? We went to prayer. Isn't that what we were supposed to do? And now YOU are supposed to FIX THIS! No intimacy, no sperm, my husband getting fat, I'm getting angry. There is NOTHING I can do with that! I have faith. I believe. I pray. But nothing, nothing! What is happening? What are You doing up there! This is not how the story is supposed to go! I'm not even asking You for anything really spectacular. Not a million dollars, not to part the Red Sea, all I need is some testosterone and a baby. We are made in Your image, right?

You have a son! Where is mine? We are supposed to be beautifully and wonderfully made. What is beautiful about this? I just want him to hold me like he used to. I want him to tell me that it's going to be okay, but my husband talks at me as if I am the problem. I wish I knew his heart and his dreams. I wish he could see mine. What didn't You tell us this before now?!?! Why God? You knew, and You know how much I want children. And him! Every time I look at his penis I get angry! Why don't You work!?!? I just want to be a good wife. I want to be a mom! I want to be a mommy! So why is this so hard! It's not hard for everyone else! HELP ME!! I don't know what to do! I want to be better. I don't understand. I know it could be worse. I'm not ungrateful. I believe. But You have to change it! CHANGE IT!!!

By the time I got done reading, the hatred in my heart had eased up a little. I can't explain why, maybe because re-reading was like venting, getting it all out in one sitting. My eyes were so puffy from crying they were nearly swollen shut. I turned off the light and sat in the darkness. I needed a break, I needed something to change for us. I was ready to leave my husband. Even the friendship we prided ourselves on was fading. Maybe we were not meant to be. Maybe I was not what he needed.

January 2

Dear Lord, I pray for my husband that You would heal his body, but most of all heal his heart. Heal my heart. Heal this marriage. Only You can mend the heart of the broken and in one second You can take this issue away, so I ask for You to continue to do work in my husband, and that his body is functioning in the perfection in which You created it to function and that there is no malfunction... continue to do a work in me so I know how to deal with this. Continue to do a work in us... I don't understand why me, why him, why us, but I guess in time maybe I will know... help me not to hate him... and I'm sorry for being angry at You... Amen.

CONFESSION: It's okay to be angry at God. In the Bible, even Job had to cover his mouth because he wanted to complain—he felt some type of way about how he was being tormented. Infertility made me finally began to understand how some people could question God's existence. Denying that I was angry at God contributed to mounting anger. What I had to do was confess how I felt. I had to scream! I had to shout! I had to tell God how I really felt about Him. He's God. He could take it. My anger was born of hurt, confusion, and disappointment. I desperately wanted a baby, and I didn't want to lose my marriage, but I didn't know what to do. There was nothing I could do to change our situation. I had no control. Every time I was at a breaking point, someone was there to either pray with me or remind me about the goodness of God. Once I acknowledged my anger, I could see that when I was at my lowest, God was there with me. And, I have to remind myself that He was always with me, even when I couldn't see Him.

Truth 11: Sharing is Caring

Semen Secret: You are the only one who is dealing with infertility. No one else knows how you feel. No one knows what it's like to be denied something you want so bad.

Conversations about kids with my friends had become awkward. The few who knew about our issue would try to be super polite. I appreciated the gesture, but it did not negate the fact that I wanted what they had. When people complained about their children or about being pregnant, I would get so angry. To complain about the very thing I wanted so desperately seemed horribly inconsiderate. Sometimes I felt that they took having a baby for granted. I wanted to remind them, *be thankful because everyone can't have a baby*. The nasty tones would often slip out before I could put them back in my mouth. My friends would follow with, "I'm sorry girl, that's not what I meant. Did I offend you?" Their apologies were genuine, but the damage had already been done, I was reminded that I still lacked what I wanted most. I would try not to roll my eyes as I smiled back and insisted it was okay. Sometimes I was the one who had to apologize when I imposed my feelings on them. My pain was my own to bear. I was alone in my world. Alone in my thoughts. I had yet to meet anyone who understood what it was like to go through what I was going through.

I hated when people with kids would try to sympathize. "I know how you feel," they would say, "I have kids, but it was still a struggle." They had no clue how I felt. They couldn't know. And I was tired of hearing, "Just stay strong." It was bullshit. "Maybe God has a different plan." What plan was that? Did his plan include giving us back the time we had already lost? Everyone tried to make me feel better, but what no one understood was that there was no feeling better. I believed my situation was an anomaly—there was no one on this earth who could empathize with me or guide me or fix it, let alone make me feel better about it.

For years I had ridden an emotional roller coaster. I would go from ranting to simmering in my feelings. I would look through social media posts from my friends and see other people's baby reveals, birth announcements, bulging bellies, and adorable babies. Then I would cry, get angry, smile, be jealous, get depressed, or curse the computer only to open it back up to look at more pictures.

One day I opened my Facebook page to begin my ritual of drowning in my sorrows and saw that one of my sorority sisters was announcing her baby. *But when was she pregnant?* I couldn't remember her being pregnant. She had a social at her house not too long ago, she didn't talk about her baby. Did I miss something?

The next day I mentioned to my husband that she had a baby, "I think she adopted it."

I thought I was against adoption, the process was brutal and it came with risks. What if the child had emotional issues? What if the kid had genetic defects and got sick? What if the adopted parents changed their mind and wanted the child back? What if the child wanted to find their real parents and left me and my husband? Adoption was terrifying the more I thought about it. Plus, I wanted to be pregnant, experience those labor pains everyone was complaining about, and most of all, hold a child in my arms who reflected me and my husband's characteristics.

But, did I want to be pregnant more than I wanted to raise a child, more than I wanted someone to call me mommy and him daddy? Month after month, my priorities changed and after seeing the Facebook post I decided that I didn't just want to be pregnant, I really wanted to have a baby. When I mentioned the post to my husband, he suggested I reach out to my sorority sister. I was shocked that he would encourage me to share our story with someone and look into adoption again, maybe his priorities were changing too.

I was nervous about calling her. We weren't close friends and we had never had a conversation more intimate than, "How are you." I almost didn't reach out to her but then, as chance would have it, I saw her at a sorority meeting and I mustered up the courage to ask her if I could give her a call. She said, "Sure," and that was that. On the way home, I rehearsed how I was going to ask her about her baby:

I didn't know you were pregnant. Too obvious, because clearly, she wasn't pregnant.

So, where did you get your baby? It sounded like I was asking her where she brought her shoes.

More worrisome than how I was gonna ask her about her baby, was how I going to tell her about my situation. Did I really want a near-stranger to know my husband's sperm didn't exist? What would she think about him? Maybe she was someone who would understand what I was going through. Maybe if I knew her situation my anxiety would go away. Which meant, I had to make the call.

What was the use of hiding behind the rawness of the pain of wanting a child when there was someone who may be able to help me get through it all? I took a deep breath and dialed her number. I was hoping she wouldn't answer, but on the third ring, I was forced to face my fear.

"Hey lady," she answered.

"Hi," I muttered, unsure of myself.

"So, what did you want to talk about?"

It's funny how you rehearse things in your head and then, when it's time to have the conversation, you just spill your guts in earnest.

"Well…umm…I wanted to ask you about your recent Facebook post. I haven't told anyone this, and I'm not sure why I'm telling you, but my husband and I have been unable to have a baby, and I told him I saw you with a baby that I think you adopted. So, he told me I should call you and find out. But you can tell me if I'm too much in your business. I'll understand."

She burst into laughter. I was trying to figure out what I said that was so funny.

"In my business? Please, I put it on Facebook. Yes, my husband and I adopted a baby girl. I always wanted a baby and after $60,000 and two failed IVF treatments, I finally have a baby girl."

I inhaled sharply, "$60,000? That is a lot of money."

"Yes, it is," she agreed. "But, when I got this baby, it was all worth it. It wasn't easy though. I've been through hell to get here. Lost my mind chile."

"I'm losing my mind too," I admitted, breathing a sigh of relief. "I torture myself with questions about why God is holding up the process. Sometimes, I try to convince myself that the delay is just giving us time to build up our finances, learn our family history, take more trips. Maybe God has a sense of humor or he is just testing my faith."

I paused, not sure I was ready to share more details, but then I didn't want to lose this opportunity to confide in someone who might finally understand. I took a deep breath and shared that my husband had no sperm.

"I always resolve that at the next doctor's appointment God will finally release the sperm and make me us parents. But I'm still waiting." My voice got a little louder as I continued, "I'm sick of people telling me to pray. Pray? I'm angry at God. Yes, angry. All women are supposed to have babies and even though they say God doesn't make bad things happen to you, the devil had to get permission from him to do so right? So that means that God saw this coming, and he didn't stop it."

I was panting, angry and feeling fully justified in my anger. She identified with the pain, the fear, the anger, the grief, even the small wins and, of course, the major defeats. She knew my story. She couldn't identify with her husband having no sperm, but she understood wanting a baby and not being able to get pregnant. Everyone else I talked to had a baby naturally. She was the first person I could talk to who could validate everything I was going through—everything I was feeling. She had gone through IVF and it did not result in a pregnancy. It was similar to my husband going through the testicular biopsy and it not resulting in any sperm. She understood what it was like for people to constantly ask when she was going to have a baby, to decline baby shower invites, to have to get over the fact that the journey to parenthood came at a cost—financially and emotionally. She understood how infertility brought turmoil in the marriage.

It felt like the weight that had been pressing on my chest had been lifted.

She joked, "Girl, I have been there and done that, brought a T-shirt, socks, and the mug! It's funny I can laugh about it now but there was a time I would cry all day. So, I'm telling you it will get better, trust that."

It's one thing for my friends and family to tell me that *it's going to be okay*, but it is completely different coming from someone who knows what it feels like when it's not okay.

She continued, "I may be 40, but I got my baby! It seems unfair, I know. This should be free. The doctors should be able to fix it all. But, if I didn't go through what I did, I wouldn't be here today trying to keep you from falling off the cliff."

Falling off the cliff? I felt like I like had jumped, landed with a sickening thud, and jumped again—several times. I kept coming back to the cliff. I'm not sure where determination left off and insanity took over.

"You can call me anytime," she offered. "Day or night, whenever the pain hits you. Whenever you're confused, call me and we can talk it through."

From then on, she was my lifeline. Every question I had about adoption, every time someone was insensitive, every time I felt empty or alone, I could call her, and she would always answer… always.

CONFESSION: There is nothing new under the sun. There is always someone who has gone through what you have been through or and those who have gone through something worse. I was not an anomaly. There was someone who knew how I felt. However, if she had never shared her story, I would have never found my comforter and confidant. I found that sharing a painful story is caring about others who may be in the same place and need to know they are not alone. I found that God will place the right people in your life when you need them the most, and often, it is a person you least expect. It was the unexpected that met my expectations. Our stories were slightly different, but our pain was similar.

Truth 12: Grief and Mourning are Different

Semen Secret: Grieving and mourning are one in the same.

For a while, I focused on trying not to focus on being pregnant. It was tough. There were days I still cried, but I made sure I did it where my husband could not see. I began to change my attitude toward my husband. I missed my friend. I wanted to talk to him, for him to talk to me. I wanted to break inside his shell and understand how he was able to cope with this heartbreak. He said he accepted that he could not have children, but I did not believe that for a second. He loved kids. There was no way he was okay with not having a family. I hadn't yet come to understand that accepting a situation and being okay with a situation were quite different. I made a vow to myself that I would no longer try to force my husband to tell me what he was feeling. When he was ready, he would open up to me.

One Sunday my husband and I had planned to do our usual: go to church and then the grocery store. This Sunday, the sermon was entitled "Forward After Crisis." The pastor explained, that to move forward after a crisis, we had to choose joy, choose trust, and choose to mourn. The Bible says, "Blessed are those who mourn, for they will be comforted," Matthew 5:4. The message ended with the imagery of a wound and the process it takes for a wound to heal. A wound that heals too quickly is only healed on the outside, not the inside. It takes time for a wound to heal.

I found myself crying through the entire message, only to turn to my right and see tears streaming down my husband's face. I wanted to hug him, but I knew at that moment something was happening inside him that I needed to let him experience alone. I had promised myself I wasn't going to cry in front of him anymore, but this cry was different. It was still sad, but peaceful.

After church, for the first time in a long time, my husband and I interacted with one another. We laughed, made jokes, and even held hands. (And, we never held hands even when we did like each other.) I made it a point to not mention I saw his tears. I knew that he kept his emotions under lock and key, but I also knew something happened inside his heart that day that changed his entire being.

Later that evening, I Googled the word "mourning" and came across several articles that explained mourning and grief as separate expressions. Grief is how a person deals with trauma and crisis on the inside. All my emotions, from anger, to shock, to sadness were all *grief*. However, *mourning* is what happens when a person takes those inside emotions and outwardly expresses them. The outward expression can show up in various forms like praying, focusing on the positives, writing in a journal, or listening to music. I had been doing this all along, journaling, listening to music, and praying (a lot of praying)—without understanding it as a therapeutic way to mourn, to heal. All this time I had been waiting for something to change inside my husband when the reality was that I also needed something to change inside of me.

That night, my husband printed the scripture my mom gave us after his surgery, Mark 11:23-24 *I tell you the truth, you can say to this mountain, 'May you be lifted up and thrown into the sea,' and it will happen. But you must really believe it will happen and have no doubt in your heart. I tell you, you can pray for anything, and if you believe that you've received it, it will be yours.*

He put it in the bathroom above our mirror and read it every day. I wanted to talk about it, but I held my tongue. This was *his* mourning process and it wasn't my place to force a conversation about it.

Over the next few weeks, I took the time to read all the things I had been writing in my journal over the past four years. That was *my* mourning process. Page after page, my writing forced me to confront my grief. Here I was, angry at the world, angry at God, hating my husband, loathing my empty womb, never understanding that I should have been dealing with myself. A month later my husband initiated a conversion about having a baby, "I've been dealing with a lot lately, and I want to let you know how all this shit makes me feels."

I gave him my full attention.

"Some days, I feel like I'm a failure," he said in a steady voice. "I've failed you, and this marriage. My goal in life is to give you the world, everything your heart desires, but the one thing I know you really want I can't give you. You know, the first two years after finding out, I thought about killing myself. Just committing suicide so that you can let go, not feel bad, and find someone who could give you what you wanted."

Committing suicide? All of this because of his inability to produce sperm? I had asked to know my husband's heart, but I was not prepared for what he revealed. *He thought about killing himself? Over children? Because of me?* Never in my wildest dreams did I think he thought about taking his own life. What would I have done had he acted on his thoughts? I had pushed him constantly, always blaming him and God for his shortcomings. All the anger and hatred I once felt melted and I was only left with a sickening guilt. I searched for the right words, but there were none. All I could say was, "I'm so sorry."

I don't know who or what kept him alive, but I was grateful. In that moment I knew that my life would hold no meaning without my husband by my side.

My heart was aching and my head was reeling. I needed to put pen to paper and journal what I was feeling and thinking. I went to the "nursery" my mom had convinced me to set up and started writing. I had to forgive myself for pushing my husband to the brink of suicide. It was one of the most humbling experiences of my life.

Though my husband and our closest family knew of my husband's condition, it was still a secret that we carried. Even I didn't know the innermost thoughts my husband had harbored or how deeply this situation had affected him. I knew he didn't want to be judged. He didn't want pity or even sympathy. He didn't want to feel less than a man. But I still believed, perhaps even more so after his recent admission, that he needed someone he could confide in. As much as I wanted him to feel comfortable confiding in me. I also understood that I wasn't a man, I couldn't identify with what it felt like for him to deal with this situation. I was worried about him carrying the weight of this burden all on his own. I asked him to talk to someone, anyone. His answer was emphatically no.

One evening as my husband and I were driving to dinner he began to open up to me out of the blue.

"You know, I want you to know how much I love you. I appreciate you and I enjoy being around you. I love you and I'm ready to really try to have children."

My heart skipped a beat and I wanted to squeal with excitement, but I stayed quiet and let him finish.

"Of course, I want it naturally. But even if it's through adoption or sperm donation, I want you to have a baby. I mean, I want us to have a baby."

I cried. Finally, they were tears of joy instead of sorrow. I had wanted to hear those words for so long. It was comforting to know that he wanted a baby too. More than anything, it eased my heart to know that he still loved me. It was a confirmation I needed. No matter what, we still cared for each other deeply. That night we were intimate in a way we hadn't been in four years. It wasn't just the physical intimacy, it was emotional and spiritual. It happened so organically, so naturally. I missed him, and he missed me.

A few months after opening up to me, my husband went on a guy's trip. I was happy that he was hanging out with friends and having fun again. It was refreshing.

During his trip he called me, "I told him."

"You told who what?" I asked, confused.

"I told someone about my issue. I told him. I just told him. I cried, and he cried with me. He told me being a dad was so much more than having a baby of my own. He told me to not let my pride get in the way of giving someone a better life. I feel so much better. I finally just got it out."

Of course, I cried. "I'm so happy for you. I'm so happy that you are finally dealing with it all. I promise I won't push you, but I want you to know that I am here with you in everything… always. I got you."

The final piece of my husband's mourning was to tell someone else—to let it go. He finally opened his heart to someone who could understand what it was like to want to be a dad. The person he talked to had experienced the ultimate grief, losing a baby in a way that took away his and his wife's ability to have a baby naturally. He could identify with my husband's fear. I didn't know why he decided to tell this guy on this day, but I did know that the hardness of his heart was softening. He could finally stop punishing himself. After I hung up the phone, I closed my eyes and took a deep breath. All those nights I prayed that he would open his heart to someone. *Even my anger at You, God, did not stop You from answering my prayer... Thanks.* It brought me back to when that he told me "God said you were going to be my wife." Of course, at the time, I didn't understand all the ins and outs of what being his wife would mean for our lives. I smiled and shook my head. We had been through so much. But, I was his wife. He was my husband.

I was relieved to know my husband hadn't given up. I didn't have to be afraid anymore that I was losing my marriage… losing my friend. Slowly, he was coming back to me. Slowly, he was coming back to *himself*. We had grieved, we had mourned, and, one-by-one, we were putting the shattered pieces of our happy life back together.

CONFESSION: It's hard to know the difference between grief and mourning. They are two separate processes and you must experience each before you can heal. I had gone through the Stages of Grief repeatedly, but I had to mourn. I needed to outwardly express my grief in ways that were positive. Sobbing over the same thing with the same people did not help me to work through my issue. I shared my grief as a way to get people to feel sorry for me, not as a way for me to talk through my hurt so I could heal. I was looking for people to tell me what I *wanted* to hear, not what I *needed* to hear. I wanted to replay my grief so I could continue to justify my feelings of anger and sadness. But it was a vicious cycle that led to more anger and sadness. I had to look myself in the mirror, put my big girl panties on, and start to engage in a process to heal my soul. The time for grieving had passed. It was time to mourn. Furthermore, I had to realize that the way I mourned and the way my husband mourned were different. We had to mourn in our own way and in our own time before we could mourn together.

Truth 13: Patience *is* a Virtue

Semen Secret: Your husband wanting a baby means he wants to have a baby right now, and by any means necessary.

As the months passed we became more open with one another. Our communication improved and every day there was a new discovery. He agreed to take the HCG injections again, in hopes of naturally increasing his testosterone and sperm count. I agreed not to get overly excited about him sharing how he was feeling. I didn't want to push him. I wanted him to feel comfortable with me.

But, I couldn't help myself.

Every week I initiated the conversation about having a baby. I sent invitations to adoption meetings. I tried to get him to schedule an appointment to do a semen analysis to see if any sperm could be found yet. I even sent subliminal messages. I bought children's books and left them on the table or when we were shopping I'd detour through the children's section of the store to look at clothes. The next year I was turning 33—the year I said I wanted to finish having children. As it stood now, I'd be lucky if I could get started by then.

I still counted down the months for imagined due dates: *If I got pregnant in September, that means I could have the baby by summer.* I downloaded an app on my phone to track my ovulation and when my phone gave me a reminder that I was ovulating, I gave my husband a nudge that we needed to have sex.

But, when you plan sex around your period, you're devastated every time your period comes back around. Therefore, every time my period came, I would lash out. My husband's willingness to try had given me a reason to hope for a child again. With that hope came expectations and those unmet expectations led to disappointment. I was spiraling again.

My emotions took control.

I desperately wanted my period to be a few days late so I could experience the excitement of taking a pregnancy test. My daydreams returned. I imagined how I would tell my husband I was pregnant, how I would reveal the pregnancy to my parents and friends, and what I would do for my baby shower. I still wanted twins, so I created catchy themes for custom shirts when we brought them home from the hospital: *Twins for the Win*. I melted every time we would talk about how we wanted to parent our kids. I was convinced that God was done testing us and my dream would soon be a reality.

Summer came to an end. Our anniversary was in a few days and it would mark eight years of marriage. Half those years we spent trying to have a baby. On that day, my husband just wanted to have a nice dinner and talk about us, our marriage, our friendship, and life in general. And, what did I want to talk about? Having a baby, of course!

"I'm just so excited about finally being able to do this! Aren't you?"

He responded flatly, "Can we talk about something else?"

Sheepishly, I changed the subject but the night remained a bit awkward. I was clueless to the idea that my husband just wanted to enjoy the moment, enjoy me. I had the nerve to be offended. I had become obsessed with my imagined future. So much so, that I was uncomfortable in the moment. I was too busy living in the future to realize that I was missing the present.

Once we got up from dinner, we went outside to take a walk. Other couples were walking together, enjoying the night as we should have been. But, I needed to understand why my husband wouldn't join me in my imagined future.

Casually, I leaned into him, looked up and asked in a soft voice, "Why did you want me to stop talking about the baby when we were at dinner?"

He turned towards me with narrowed eyes, "You know what your problem is?" He said in a forced whisper. "You are impatient. You jump from one thing to the next. You can't wait for anything."

I took a step back.

"I was laying on a hospital bed with my dick cut open, and you asked me when we were gonna adopt." The veins above his eyebrows were bulging now.

"Now, I open up to you a little bit and you wanna talk about babies every day. What's wrong with you? You can't let go of this time table. You are consumed with this baby stuff. I understand that this may take a long time, or it may never happen at all. But what I'm not gonna do is try to force something. I can't consume my life with this every day.

"We have to live!" he shouted.

He lowered his voice, "Stop trying to force this. Just let whatever will happen, happen. Take a break from this shit."

My face crumpled, but I tried to hold back the tears. He looked up the sky and took a deep breath, then turned back and held my hand.

"Look, I want a baby and want to be a father." I could see the sincerity in his eyes. "But talking about it every moment of every day of your life is not going to bring the baby here any faster. I really wish it could, for my sake and yours. You are the one always talking about faith and waiting on God, but you're not even doing it yourself."

I was exposed. I wanted to hide. He was right. I was impatient. But I was also scared. Faith required bravery. I hid behind my tears and told him he was being mean. Outwardly, I blamed him for the shame I was feeling. Internally, I blamed myself. Where *was* my faith?

Why was I so willing to give up the present for an uncertain future? I couldn't answer those questions.

My parents always said that when we go through valley situations, "You shouldn't ask God, 'When are you going to bring me out?' You should be asking 'What do you want me to learn in this season?'" Maybe God wanted to teach me something about waiting. But, my season had been so long... four years! I'm not saying that God caused my husband's infertility, but maybe through this situation, God wanted me to learn something.

When we got home I ran upstairs to the nursery to wallow in my sad truth. Life was passing me by because I was so consumed with a baby and semen—two things that didn't even exist for me. I was driving myself into madness. I never paused. After every failed attempted at conception I began searching for an alternative way to have a baby. I covered one scar with another, packing wound on top of wound with not attempt to ever heal. I never directly dealt with the individual situation or stopped to check the pulse of how each new drama made us feel.

I hated the fact that my husband pointed out my hypocrisy. But it was exactly what I needed to hear.

CONFESSION: Moving from one thing to the next was unhealthy, and downright unnerving. It was my way of avoiding dealing with my pain. My impatience was linked to my unwillingness to let go of how I thought our journey to parenthood was supposed to go. I had forsaken my faith and I was relying on me, and me alone, to get my baby. I did not take time to accept that I didn't have the power or the ability to make this baby happen for us. My time table was important to me, but it was arbitrary in the big picture. I wanted to live up to society's expectation that my husband and I have a baby naturally. I was so determined and narrow-minded about when and how it should happen that I was insensitive to my husband and his condition. I linked our parents getting older, the health of my marriage, even my sense of worth, all on a baby. I wasn't content with loving parents, a doting husband, loyal friends. I only wanted what I didn't have, and I neglected what I did have. It was sobering to finally process this fact: patience was a virtue I just didn't have. It was something I had to acquire with time.

Truth 14: Husband before Children... Always

Semen Secret: Your desire to have a child is more important than your husband because if you two had a child, you would both be happy and your marriage would be whole.

I was overcome with guilt. I was supposed to be the Christian woman holding up her husband. But, I was the hypocrite. I wasn't sure how to deal with who I had become. I wasn't sure how to reconcile my desire to have a child with my faith, considering I was unable to have a child. How could I trust what was not promised to me? How could I continue to believe when all the times I did believe, I had been disappointed?

The answer came to me, and it was my husband.

I will never forget Halloween of that year. We had come home from a friend's party and the night had been good. Good friends, good food, good drinks, good time. We retreated to our basement to spend the remainder of the evening listening to music, drinking, and dancing in our costumes. It was something we hadn't done in a while. He was the mixologist, I was the DJ. We sat on the sofa to make a toast and he laid his head on my stomach. It was an odd gesture.

"What are you doing?" I asked.

"I'm listening for a heartbeat."

Then he kissed my stomach, clinked my glass, and said, "Cheers to our future."

I was undone. *He loved me despite my hypocrisy? Despite my impatience? Regardless of the pressure I put him under?* The moment gave me a profound understanding of unconditional love. Love is more than happily ever after. Love was our anger, our tears, our pain, and even our shortcomings. Love found a way to make us vulnerable and allow us to rediscover its true meaning.

Despite all the heartache I had caused my husband by blaming him or rushing him, he was still my friend. He knew I needed to see him believe so my faith could again be restored. I'm not sure he believed in what he was saying, but it was his step of faith that kept me going, that allowed me to begin to forgive myself.

The next month we got a call from his aunt saying she knew a girl who wanted to find a family to adopt her baby. I was excited, but I couldn't take another heartbreak, so I kept my expectations in check. And, as I had assumed, the girl never got back to us. We entered the holiday season—already a rough time for us—and learned that at least five more couples in our circle of friends were expecting babies. I was devastated, and my husband saw my defeat. He loved on me more than he had to, more than I would know how to do if the shoe were on the other foot. He accepted that I was broken, and he treated me gently. I knew he had the issue, and he knew I was the one dealing with it.

The week before Christmas, we were cleaning up and found a onesie for a little boy stuffed in a drawer. It said *Mommy's Little Dude*. I burst into tears, but my husband just smiled. I wasn't sure why, but at that moment I felt a profound sense of peace. We didn't remember buying or being gifted the onesie. Neither of us could explain where it came from, but it was a reminder that God had not forgotten us.

That evening, while he was asleep, I got up and I walked upstairs to the "nursery." I replayed all that we had endured. I was drawn to 1 Peter 3:1-2: *Likewise, wives, be subject to your own husbands, so that even if some do not obey the word, they may be won without a word by the conduct of their wives, when they see your respectful and pure conduct.* As usual, I cried, aware of my shortcomings. My restlessness continued, as did my revelations. I read through my journal hoping that would put me to sleep. I ran across sermon notes on priorities in marriage: God, Husband, Children. Children were listed last. They came after my marriage. I paused to consider this. Number three: Children. Number two: Husband—only after God.

It was so clear. I was out of priority. I put a child, rather the possibility of a child, before my husband. I even put semen before my husband. If I was doing this now, what would I do when we did have a baby. I was so focused on this non-existent baby, that I failed to focus on my very present husband. Even if we had children, once they were all grown and out the house, the world would return to just us two. If we didn't nurture and build our marriage without children, how were we going to survive with them?

I had been so concerned with my desire for children that I failed to focus on my marriage, my husband, and his well-being. He could be sick for the rest of his life and I had dismissed that. His low testosterone could lead to osteoporosis and even shorten his life expectancy. He sacrificed his health for my desires and I glossed over that in my pursuit to be a mother. To please me, he endured multiple tests, surgery, and experimental drugs. He did this because I wanted a baby. I let semen become more important that the man I'd loved for nearly half my life. I shocked myself. How could I be so inconsiderate?

CONFESSION: I needed my husband. He needed me. We two, that's all that existed. But, at the rate I was going, it was going to be just me. This new sense of awareness was not for him. It was for me. This was my continued process of mourning. I had put the desire for my child before my husband. My priorities were out of order and out of line with the way God designed marriage. The time I spent focusing on trying to have my children, I should have been spending trying to cultivate my marriage… supporting my husband. I had clearly failed this lesson.

Truth 15: Accept Reality

Semen Secret: There can be no reality in a marriage that does not include a baby.

We were in year four of our journey through infertility. January started off with the urologist telling us that there was nothing left he could do for my husband to raise his testosterone in hopes of producing sperm.

"Your husband does produce sperm, but they just stop growing after a point. I can't explain why. You really need to think about other ways to have children."

This was the point in the conversation where I would usually break down in tears, but not this time.

I smiled, "Thank you, doctor, for all you have tried to do. When we become parents, I'll make sure to bring the baby back to shake your hand."

The doctor smiled back and so did my husband. Even though we didn't have the results we had hoped for, there was a relief knowing that our visits to the urologist were over. The medication had caused my husband to become weak and gain weight. I hated seeing him like that and we were both happy to move forward…even if we didn't know what was ahead of us.

One Sunday we stayed home to watch church service online. Service at our church starts with praise and worship and then a prayer for healing. As we bowed our heads to pray, our pastor's wife, who is also a pastor, began to pray for healing.

"There is someone listening to the sound of my voice desiring to have a child. You have been waiting for a while, but God wants you to know He hasn't forgotten about you."

My husband and were in disbelief. I don't even remember what the sermon was about that day, all I did was replay what she said repeatedly. The old me would have started trying to get pregnant before church service even ended, but the resolved me just made a mental note. I took comfort knowing God had not forgotten about me.

The next month we got a phone call from a family friend saying that her sister-in-law had a little boy she was fostering who would soon be up for adoption because his birth mother did not have the capacity to take care of him. I had long ago gotten over my hesitation about adoption, but to get this child we would have to go through the foster parent process before we could adopt. We went to an interest meeting and filled out the background paperwork to begin the process of doing another home study and taking classes as required by the state. Given that the baby would be up for adoption soon, we wanted to expedite the process. We reached out to the current foster parent to provide her with pictures and information she could give the mother and the caseworker who was responsible for the child. She sent us pictures of the little boy and, though my husband had been adamant that he only wanted a little girl, the possibility of having a little person running around our house superseded those desires. We both allowed ourselves to get excited.

While we were getting our paperwork together, I called the foster mother every week to get an update on the child. As time passed, however, we started receiving fewer updates. Then the process with the home study stalled because we had a pool in our backyard and would need to fence in the pool structure. Eventually, we stopped hearing from the foster mother, and soon thereafter we stopped pursuing the adoption altogether. Again. It was sad for us both. However, this time it did not hurt as bad as the others. Surprisingly, we were okay with it all. Our experiences had taught us that denial was a part of the risk we had to take on the path to parenthood.

The failed adoption led us to have an honest discussion about what we wanted. How did we want to move forward? This was the third time we had considered adoption. We agreed we weren't ready to consider a sperm donor, and we did not want my husband to go through surgery again. We reconciled that our road to parenthood would be someone giving us a baby, adopting, or continuing to wait on our miracle. In the meantime, we could continue to cry, be mad, argue, and be jealous about the fact that we were not parents, or we could focus our energies on other aspects of our life and our marriage that we could work on until we became parents.

We began to accept that whatever was going to happen with us being parents was completely out of our control. It was heartbreaking, but we realized that we may never become parents. I was terrified of the question, *what if I never become a mommy?* We decided that even though the situation was beyond our control, we didn't have to give up on our dreams to have children. We agreed we would still talk about what we would do with our kids. We would call them by name. We would even talk about where they would sleep and the types of things they would do. What we wouldn't do was let these children we already loved so much stop us from living our lives, from loving each other.

Looking back over our marriage, we were glad we didn't have any children around to see us at our worst. We had been terrible to one another. We had to learn how to be married. We had to learn each other. Infertility was the best teacher.

A few days after accepting our new reality, I finally let go of my timetable and told my husband I wanted him to reach back out to the urologist so he could begin taking synthetic testosterone.

"But you remember what the doctor said, right? That if I start taking this then it could eliminate our chances of having a baby naturally?"

I understood it all. I knew he would hold out as long as possible to help us achieve our dream. Yet, I couldn't keep putting his health on hold for this baby.

"I know what the doctor said, but I've been seeing you looking a little more tired every day. You're not supposed to have testosterone levels this low. The doctor also said, every day you are not on some type of treatment, you lower your life expectancy. If I can't have a baby crying and keeping me awake at night, I need you around to get on my nerves. I want you to know that I'm ok with it all. I just want you to feel better. That's what is most important right now."

He was surprised by my willingness to let go of natural childbirth for his sake. I surprised myself. It felt good to let him know that I loved him more than motherhood. I wanted him to know I would put him first, above all else. He needed to know that. Testosterone was necessary to make sure he was going to be able to live a healthy life, especially since no one could explain why his levels were low in the first place. In just a month after taking his medication, his health improved exponentially. He wasn't tired and sluggish, he felt better, and his sex drive gave us new reasons to enjoy our marriage.

I knew that each day he was on the medication was a day deleted from our ability to have children naturally, but I realized that I wanted to spend my complete life with him. My children would eventually leave the house to live their lives. My husband was my only constant.

He would always have to be second to God, but first before my children. When we would finally become parents, my life would still begin and end with the one who gave me a ring and professed to God that he would love me forever.

CONFESSION: This story ends with my husband and I still wanting a baby. My truth is that every day I hold on to the hope that, one day, someone will call me mommy and call him daddy. We keep all our options open: from pregnancy, to adoption, to a miracle. But for now, we embrace the things we have in front of us. We have the gift of time and space that we may not have had if we had children. For years we ignored that freedom. I viewed it as a curse. I wasted years watching the clock tick by with our parents getting older, my husband getting sicker, and my womb continuing to be empty.

Do we get sick and tired of people asking us, *when you gonna have some babies?* Of course! People don't understand that a question which seems so harmless can pour salt on a wound that has been open and bleeding for a long time. Yet, I have to give people the benefit of the doubt and realize that their expectation of parenthood is the same one I held on to for a very long time.

I would be lying if I said there weren't days that we still asked *why us?* There are still days we cry and get frustrated at our situation. Yet, there are other days when we say *why not us?* I believe there is a blessing in what we have gone through both as individuals and as a couple. The things that could have broken us, that should have broken us, made us stronger. We don't have everything we want, but we do have everything we *need*. We have the love, devotion, kindness, understanding, empathy, sympathy, laughter, faith, and spirit to carry each other through this thing we call life. We have the opportunity to explore, to work on us, to give, to travel, to build knowledge, to help others, to expand our talents, increase our faith, to strengthen our spirit, and grow our wealth—all so that, when the time comes, we can leave a legacy for our children. We can say we did not give up on each other nor our faith that we will one day achieve our dream.

The secret in the semen was that it wanted us to confess who we really were. It got us to a place where we were raw and vulnerable, where we could no longer hide behind the facade of being the perfect couple. We were broken down to the weakest part of our being and our marriage. We had nothing else to lean on but ourselves and God. I don't know the kind of people we would be had this secret been revealed too early or never existed at all. What I do know is that I am in love with my husband, with who we are, and where we are going… even without a baby!

About the Author

I am not TJ Peyten. *TJ* and *Peyten* are the names I want to give my children. I refrain from using the past tense, "wanted," because I still hold on to the hope that my husband and I will achieve our dream of becoming parents.

I write as TJ Peyten because it is the desire to conceive them that led to the discovery of the "Semen Secrets." If it were not for our longing to bring them into this world, there would be no story to tell. I chose to write with a pen name because our story is still ongoing, our struggle is still an everyday event, and we're still learning to cope with these Secrets and the Truths they have revealed.

As for me, I am like almost all married women who desire to conceive a child with her husband. My husband and I are like many married couples trying to navigate life, love, and marriage one day at a time.

I have written thousands of stories in my journal over the years, but this is the first one I've been brave enough to share with the world. In sharing my story, I hope that I can help someone else who is struggling to accept the unacceptable.

Semen Secrets

www.ingramcontent.com/pod-product-compliance
Lightning Source LLC
Chambersburg PA
CBHW071154090426
42736CB00012B/2326